RURAL AREA DEVELOPMENT IN BIHAR

Dr. Nilotpal Kumar

RAJESH PUBLICATIONS
NEW DELHI - 110 002

Published by :
Sanjay Gupta
RAJESH PUBLICATIONS
1, Ansari Road, Darya Ganj
New Delhi - 110002
Ph.: 011-23274550, 43084725
Email : rajeshpublications@gmail.com
Website : www.rajeshpublications.com

First Published in India 2020

ISBN : 978-81-94426-98-1

Price : Rs. 800.00

Printed in India by :
Belwel Process
Delhi-110002

Dedicated

to My Mother

Late Urmila Devi

Foreword

I feel immense pleasure to write down the forwarding of the book "Rural Area Development in Bihar" written by Dr. Nilotpal Kumar. This book deals with the important aspects of Rural Area development. It is the need of time. India is the country of villages. Almost its 67.00% population live in the village. They are Lagging behind in the race of development. Without their development. The development of the nation is a distant dream. Therefore Father of the nation Mahatma Gandhi paid his attention on rural development. After Independence Lal Bahadur Shastri, Mrs. Indira Gandhi and Dr. A.P.J. Abdul Kalam paid their attention on rural area development of India. Author of this book also tried his best to describe rural area development.

There are 9 (Nine) Chapters in this book. Chapter 1 consisting of Area and extent, significance of study, choice of study, methodology and sources of data and maps. Chapter 2 deals with geographical personality. Chapter 3 deals with demographic features, Chapter 4 deals classification of land, Chapter 5 deals with general pattern of landuse, Chapter 6 consists of growth centres, Chapter 7 deals with Rural area development, Chapter 8 deals with Planning of the Countryside and Chapter 9 deals Summary and Conclusion.

This book is well supported by tables, maps and diagrams. It also contains very informative bibliography. I hope that this book will be very useful for the students, scholars, teachers, planners, social workers of different disciplines. At the end I congratulate Dr. Nilotpal Kumar with great pleasure for his highly appreciable and scholarly deads.

Dr. Radheshyam Prasad
Former Head and Associate Professor
Dept. of Geography
Ram Krishna Dwarika College
Lohiyanagar, Patna - 20

Preface

Since Independence India has embarked upon comprehensive national development and in this endeavour rural resurgence has got prepoderance because of the fact that overwhelming population of India live in villages. Our 70% population live in villages and almost 65% of them involved in agricultures and various rural industries.

Five Year plans aimed at uplifting economic as well as socio-cultural conditions of the rural areas has had marginal success. We are now able to attain self sufficiency in food production. Growth in industries has been phenomenal. But inspite of these achievements our basic problems of poverty and unemployment still continues to afflict us. 'Rural development' is the only panacea for these problems which are hindrances in the way of making India a developed country.

The present work entitled "**Rural Area Development in Bihar**" is outcomes of my research "Rural Area Development : A Geographical Analysis of Vaishali District, Bihar", Introspects the conditions of economic and socio-cultural development of Vaishali district as well as potentiality of rural development in the region.

The present book incorporates Nine chapters including Summary and conclusion. In addition there are twenty four maps and several tables.

Chapter I : Introduces the area with a note its significance of the study, choice of study project, methodology, sources of data, sources of maps etc.

Chapter II : Outline landforms, geology, structure, drainage, rivers, climate, seasons, climatic control on agricultural landuse natural vegetation, soils, factors influencing soil, development of soil profiles and water resources etc.

Chapter II : Analysis Socio–cultural framework of the district viz. Population growth and distribution, occupational structure etc.

Chapter IV : Define land classification and quality of land in the region.

Chapter V : Analysis General pattern of landuse, variety and intensity of crops, crop combination and agricultural efficiency.

Chapter VI : Deals with Growth Centres of the area and methodology of study.

Chapter VII : Defines rural area development and Illustrates economic and socio-cultural developments of the area.

Chapter VIII : Deals with Basic Principles of Plannning and proposes changes in general landuse and management of wasteland.

Chapter IX : Concludes with the Summary and Conclusion.

Dr. Nilotpal Kumar

Acknowledgement

I express my deep sense of gratitude to my supervisor Dr. Radheshyam Prasad, Head, Department of Geography, R.K.D. College, Lohiyanagar, Patna-20 for his peerless guidance and invaluable suggestions to shape this book.

I Would like to express my gratitude to Dr. Ram Lagan Prasad, Lecturer, Deptt. of Geography, R.K.D. College, Prof. C.D. Mahato, Ex-Principal, R.K.D College and Dr. Ganesh Prasad, Ex-Head, Deptt. of Hindi, B.R.A. University, Muzaffarpur for their timely suggestions and inspiration. It is my moral duty to place on record the love and afffection as well as encouragement offered to me by my parents Dr. Jagat Narayan Sinha (Father), Head, Deptt. of Hindi, and Prof. Incharge, R.K.D. College, Lohiyanagar, Patna and Late Urmila Devi (Mother) whose blessings enabled me to accomplish this book. I am indebted to my caring wife Anjali Krishna, daughter Malvika Krishna and son Yuvraj Krishna, whose love and belief in me inspired me to accomplish this task.

I am also thankful to those learned authors whose precious views have been incorporated in this book. At last, I would like to thank all Villagers and individuals who helped me by away of giving advice and views for the preparation of this book.

Patna **Dr. Nilotpal Kumar**

Email: dr.nilukrishna@gmail.com

Contents

List of Maps and Diagrams

1

Introduction

The area under study is the administrative unit of Northern Bihar called Vaishali District. It is situated between 25°3' N and 26°N Latitudes and 85°04' and 85°38 longitudes. The district Vaishali is the part of old Muzaffarpur disrict. It became a full fledged district in the year 1972, when it was separated from Muzaffarpur district. Its area is 2036 sq.km wherever, population is 2718389 persons (2001) while 3495021 in 2011 census. It is demarcated by Muzaffarpur in the North, the river Ganga in the south, Samastipur in the east, wherever river Gandak in the west.

The districts has sixteen anchals which are following : Hajipur (137.12 sq.km), Lalganj (151.43 sq.km), Vaishali (126.81 sq.kms), Patedi Belsar (74.16 sq.kms), Bhagwanpur (118.28 sq.kms), Goraul (98.88 sq.kms), Chehra kalan (68.31 sq.kms), Patepur (256.57 sq.kms), Mahua (140.03 sq.kms), Jandaha (150.32 sq.kms), Raja pakar (75.57 sq.Km), Raghopur (225.80 sq.kms), Bidupur (114.54 sq.kms), Desri (49.99 sq.kms), Sahdai Bujurg (87.74 sq.kms), Mahnar (89.87 sq.kms).

The Vaishali district is the part of the extensive middle Ganga plain. It is drained by the mighty river Ganga and its tributary river Gandak which comes from the Himalayan zone with a heavy load of debries. Since these river are in their old stages of the cycle of erosion, they are a gradational in character. This property of the river has influenced the landuse pattern of the area from time of time.

Vaishali district makes a separate entity with regard to its cultural landscape. It forms a zone of transition among cultural regions of Mithila, Magadh and Bhojpur. Thus it has developed into a mixed cultural zone having impact of the traits of Mithila, Magadh and Bhojpur regions. The local dialect called 'vajjika' reflects the impact of all the above mentioned cultures.

The area under study was elevated to the status of a district in 1972 AD. Prior to this date, it formed part of the old Muzaffarpurs district. The Muzaffarpur district was itself a part of Tirhut district till 1875 A.D. The historical records inhabited and ruled by great men and famous kings during different historical periods. During early vedic period, the area was occupied by the Aryans.

As the 'Ramayana' and 'purana' Hindu mythological records show Vaishali was a seperate Kingdom founded by 'Raja Vishala'. The religious literatures of Jainism and Buddhism also have descriptions of this area. Lord Mahavira was born in this area. It is said that he was born in 'kundpura' or 'kunda grama' a suburb of Vaishali. Buddhist literatures mentions 'kotigrama' a place where lord Budha gave sermons to 'Ambpali' and licchavis of Vaishali. It seems that the 'Kotigrama' of Buddhists literature is identical to 'Kundagrama' of Jain literature.

The growth of the patliputra kingdom on the bank of the Ganga had a great impact upon the area (Vaishali). King Ajatsatru of Magadh annexed it to his kingdom. The famous Chinese traveller Fa-hien visited this area during reign of Chandragupta II. Another Chinese Hiuen-Tsang come to Vaishali in 635 A.D. This chinese traveller has given a very good account of the state of affairs prevalent in that period in Vaishali.

According to Huen Tsang, the area was agriculturally very rich and produced a number of crops. The area was rich and fertile. Its climate was excellent enough to grow various crops.

Ghyasuddin Tughlaq invaded this area in 1324 A.D. and put an end to the local dynasty of king Simraon. In this way the area became a part of the empire of Delhi. It was handed over to Rameshwar Thakur, the founder of the 'Sugauna dynasty' which ruled this area till the early part of the 16th century. 'Hajipur' name was derived from Haji Ilyas who was a king of Bengal (1345-50 AD). Hajipur was strategic city situated on the confluence of the Gandak and the Ganga. It was the headquarter of the governor and rulers of Bengal.

With the transfer of headquarter to Patna the importance of Hajipur, However declined considerably. In 1764 A.D. when British became victorious at Buxar, the whole of Bihar came under British rule. The area was very fertile but the rivers flooded it every year. The area become pioneer in indigo cultivation during British rule. Even some sugar factories were converted into indigo industrial units. However cultivation of sugarcane was also given proper attention by the Britishers.

In 1875 AD Muzzaffarpur was separated from Darbhanga District and became an independent district. At that time Vaishali, the present district was the subdivision of old Muzaffarpur district and was also known as Hajipur subdivision.

The earthquake of 1934 is the greatest calamity experienced till this date. Though there had been immense loss of life and property but removed the unhygienic congestions and converted the area into a cleaner and healthier one. With the beginning of the present century Vaishali could not remain isolated from nationalist movement. There had been a wide and strong response during the 'Non-Cooperation' movement and 'Civil disobedience' movement for the attainment of freedom. In 1942 during 'Quit India movement' the people of Vaishali district played important role and took active part. They highly responded to the call of Mahatma Gandhi.

After the attainment of freedom in 1947 AD the area has undergone remarkable improvement and there has been an alround progress in several respect. The Hajipur subdivision of Muzaffarpur district acquired the status of an independent district in 1972. It was named 'Vaishali' with its headquarter at 'Hajipur'. The ancient glory of the area has declined to a great extent. However, the state government has taken several measures of development. The formation of community development blocks is one of the steps taken in this regard.

The development plans are being executed through these development blocks. The recent construction of 'Mahatma Gandhi Setu' across the river Ganga has linked this area directly to the state capital Patna. This bridge will go a long way in promoting the progress of 'Vaishali' district.

Significances and choice of the project :

Since Independence India has embarked upon comprehensive national development and in this endeavour rural resurgence has got preponderance because of the fact that over-whelming population of India live in villages and all round problems there are not only pathetic but also more pervasive. The realization has been that without rural reconstruction national development will simply be fatuation. Efforts at socio-economic transformation led to several reorientations. The administration had to come out of regulatory clutches and transform it to development mould. The planning process also required economic renovation and new initiative and direction in the changing context. Community development programme (CDP) as a part of first five year plan was launched in 1952 as a concept and method for rural development. Development blocks were created for agricultural improvement. Operationally the programme was not, however, spearheaded by the community itself but by the administrative machinery. All in all this was 'governmental programme to assist people and not viceversa. The succesive plans aimed at amounting the problems of poverty unemployment and social development has yielded fruits. We are now able to attain self–sufficiency in food production. Growth in industries had been so phenomenal that we are not the tenth most industrialized country in the world. But inspite of this our basic problems of poverty of our population is still living under the rigours of poverty and starvation. Problems of unemployment has become more acute over the years. At the beginning of the sixth five year plan 12 million persons were without employment. Even today, more than 20,000 people are reportedly joining the queue of job seekers, daily during the tenth five year plan. Despite the commendable objectives these programmes could not transformation of the rural economy.

'Rural development' is the only panacea for the above ever growing problems which are hindrances in the way of making India a developed country. As 70% of its people reside in villages and almost 65% of the population is involved in agriculture and various rural industries. Gram Swaraj theory of rural development propounded by Gandhiji aimed at Upliftment of village people through self government and self employment. The village cottage industries, animal husbandry, agriculture and decentralized administration at village panchayats were some of the tools propunded by his for rural development.

The Choice of Study project :

Bihar lives in her villages with 74% of population residing in villages. Vaishali district truly represents Bihar in that respect. The study of rural development in Vaishali district would certainly give introspect to the rural development in Bihar and eventually our country. Today rural development has become a catch word in academic and planning organization circles. For the present study this term has been used as a view in very process of planning and implementation of rural development. Rural development is a strategy to improve the socio-economic life of people in the rural areas by bringings about the necessary institutional and attitudinal changes for the development of agriculture and rural industries and also for the establishment of services in the area of health, education and employment. The term 'Rural development refers not only for economic progress but also for the task of achieving the goals of plan objectives such as social justice, eradication of untouchability and women empowerment to bring the desired change in outlook of people by translating the community decisions into action through village panchayats. Myrdal in his historic book "Asian Drama" has pointed out that if we are able to secure development with social justice, we can usher in a new era of development. The present study may also prove useful in the development programme of the area in respect of agriculture industries and social structure of the villages as well.

METHODOLOGY :

In the present work an attempt has been made to study and analyse the changing pattern of Rural Developments through a systematic approach based on a firm statistical footing. The area chosen for the purpose is Vaishali districts of Bihar state and the census year 1991 and 2001 have been selected for data interpretation at blocks and district level. The relevant data and figures have been made available from the Department of Statistics and evaluation govt. of Bihar, Patna.

The candidate did intensive field work to get the real facts. Frequent visits to the field provide some salient clues to overcome the round information and their irrelevant translation on the map. All the significant data and regional characteristics have beens mapped by a suitable cartographic technique. It has been rightly remarked that "any data that can not be subjected to cartography analysis may not be treated to be geographical"

So far as the genera geography of the region is concerned, on the physical side, attempt has been made to study the physical features of all the physical aspect of the region and on economic and cultural side, anchal level maps, figures and data have been prepared. As agricultlure is the backbone and main source of the rural economy. Study gives emphasis on the agricultural features such as landuse pattern, distribution of crops, cropping patterns; social factors of population growth, distribution and occupational structure have also been analysed.

Table 1.1
Vaishali District 2001

Name of the anchal	Area in sq. kms^2	Total Population 2001	Total Population 2011
1. Vaishali	126.81	146364	187486
2. Patheri Belsan	74.16	74461	95669
3. Lalganj	151.00	203729	228286
4. Bhagwanpur	118.28	162213	207762
5. Goraul	98.88	135502	177586
6. Chehra Kelan	68.31	100828	131004
7. Patepur	256.57	282845	370182
8. Mahua	140.03	218344	284526
9. Jandaha	150.32	207837	276217
10. Raja Pakar	75.57	120221	158130
11. Hajipur	137.22	349694	296288
12. Raghopur	225.80	187722	232909
13. Desri	49.99	77741	87606
14. Sahdai Bujurg	87.74	99459	127396
15. Mahnar	89.87	144040	132046
Vaishali	**2036**	**2718421**	**3495021**

Source : Self computation based on available data.

References :

1. Stamp L.D. : The land of Britain, its use and misuse, IInd Ed. 1950.
2. Marsh, G.P. : Man and Nature, Physical Geography as modified by human action, 1864.
3. Singh, R.L. (1960) : Geographical concepts and methods of research work, National Geographical society of India, Varanasi, vol. VI, Part 3, p. 135.
4. Shafi, M. : Techniques of rural landuse and planning in India, The Geography, vol. XIII, 1966.
5. Chatterjee, S.P. : Department of Geography university of Kolkata, Progress of Geography. Fifty years of Science in India.

6. Shafi M. : Land utilization in Uttar Pradesh, 1960, Preface P. VII.
7. Diwakar R. (1950) : Bihar through the ages.
8. Jacobi, H. : Sacred Books of the east.
9. District Gazetteer of Muzaffarpur.
10. Singh, R.L. (1960) : India : A regional geography, N.G.S.I. Varanasi, p. 208.
11. Bihar through figures, 1992, Govt. press, Gulzarbagh, Patna.
12. Provisional population totals census of India 2001, series 11, Bihar, p. 27.
13. Singh, R. P. and Kumar Anil (1970) : Monograph of Bihar" Bharti Bhawan publication, Patna.
14. Dayal, P : Bihar in maps.
15. District census handbook of Vaishali, 1991 & 2001.
16. Topographical sheets of the survey of India, Dehradun.
17. District map of Vaishali published by the survey of India, 1979.
18. Cadastals map of anchals, published by Govt. of Bihar, Gulzarbagh, Patna.

2

Geographical Personality

Geographical personality of the area under study is most important part. It incorporates into it not only physical features but human aspects as well. As man is the Master of Environment but the physical factors also exert influence over the socio-economic development of man. Major factors of the physical environment is relief or, landform, geology, climate, drainage pattern, natural vegetation and soil etc.

Geology :

Vaishali is a part of the middle Ganga plain or North plain of Bihar. Thus it is composed of thick alluvium. Alluvium consist of a mixture of gravel, sand, loam and silt in varying proportions. It has been deposited by the tributaries of the Ganga. In fact, the area is a part of the 'Indo-Gangetic trough' which has been filled up by the alluvium brought down by the Himalayan rivers as well as peninsular rivers coming from South to North. As a result, the whole area has been transformed into a gently slopping plain. The famous geologist 'Oldham' has estimated this plains thickness to be 4572 mts. while 'Dunn' who has done considerable work on Indian geology observes that the thickness may be of unknown depth.

The following table gives an account of the Lithological arrangements at varying depths as observed from the record of the soil bores on the northern end fo the "Mahatma Gandhi Setu".

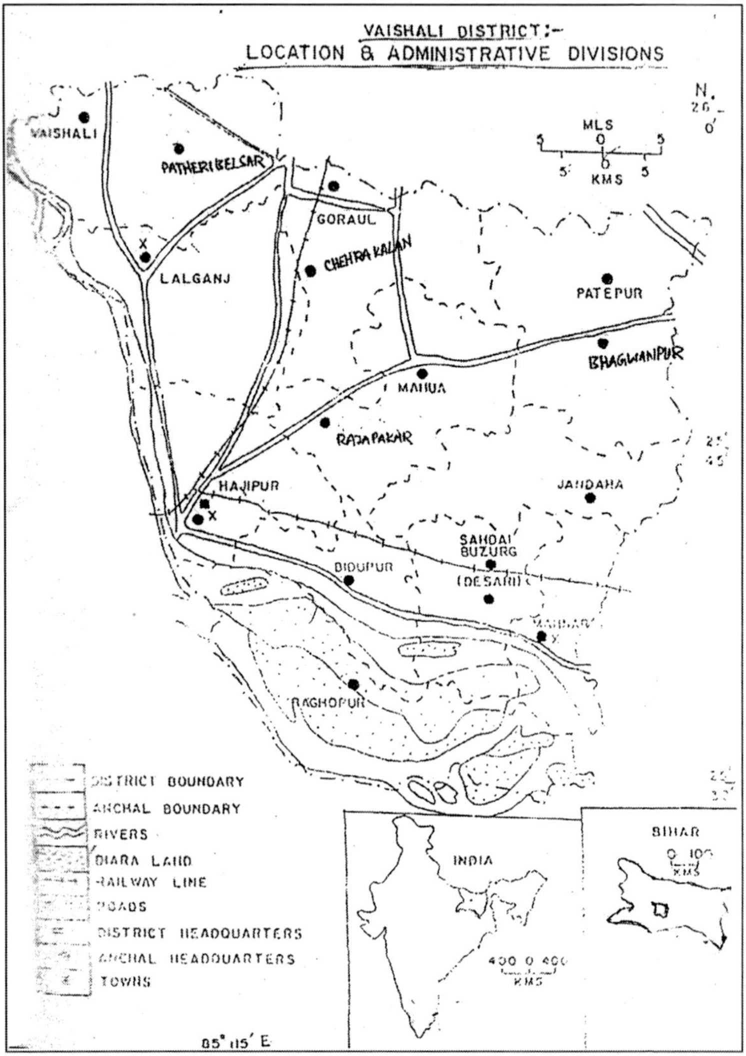
VAISHALI DISTRICT :-
LOCATION & ADMINISTRATIVE DIVISIONS
N.
MLS
KMS
VAISHALI
PATHERI BELSAR
GORAUL
LALGANJ
CHEHRA KALAN
PATEPUR
BHAGWANPUR
MAHUA
RAJAPAKAR
HAJIPUR
JANDAHA
SAHDAI BUZURG
BIDUPUR
(DESARI)
RAGHOPUR
DISTRICT BOUNDARY
ANCHAL BOUNDARY
RIVERS
DIARA LAND
RAILWAY LINE
ROADS
DISTRICT HEADQUARTERS
ANCHAL HEADQUARTERS
TOWNS
INDIA
BIHAR
85° 15' E

Fig. 2.1

Table 2.1
Vaishali : Lithological arrangement

Depth in Mtr.	Lithological arrangement
0–25	Clay with Kankar
25–30	Sand
30–35	Clay with kankar

Source : Ganga bridge at Patna, A PWD report 1981.

Landforms :

Main landform of the area are result of the differential deposition and the meandering character of the rivers. The general slope is from North-west to South-east as indicated by the course of the rivers. The contour map drawn on an interval of two meters gives fair idea of the relief of the region. The north-western side is the highest while the south-eastern section of the district is the lowest. The highest value of the contour is 52 mtrs. Whereas the lowest value is 40 mtrs, thus giving the area a landform of only 12 mtrs. The contour shows very gentle slope except the Goraul anchal where slope is very stup.

The area lying south to this contour has a very gentle slope. This area consists mainly the parts of Raghopur anchal, which is formed of diara tracts. The height of this region is hardly 44 mtrs. The maximum height is observed in the vaishali anchal in the North-west where it is more than 50 mtrs. The relief of the Vaishali district has been carried out by the expansion of alluvial fans of the river Gandak.

On the basis of the micro features the study area can be divided into three areas of subdued relief. These features are the result of the differential alluviation by the rivers. These are (1) Higher areas, (2) Intermediate areas, (3) Lower areas.

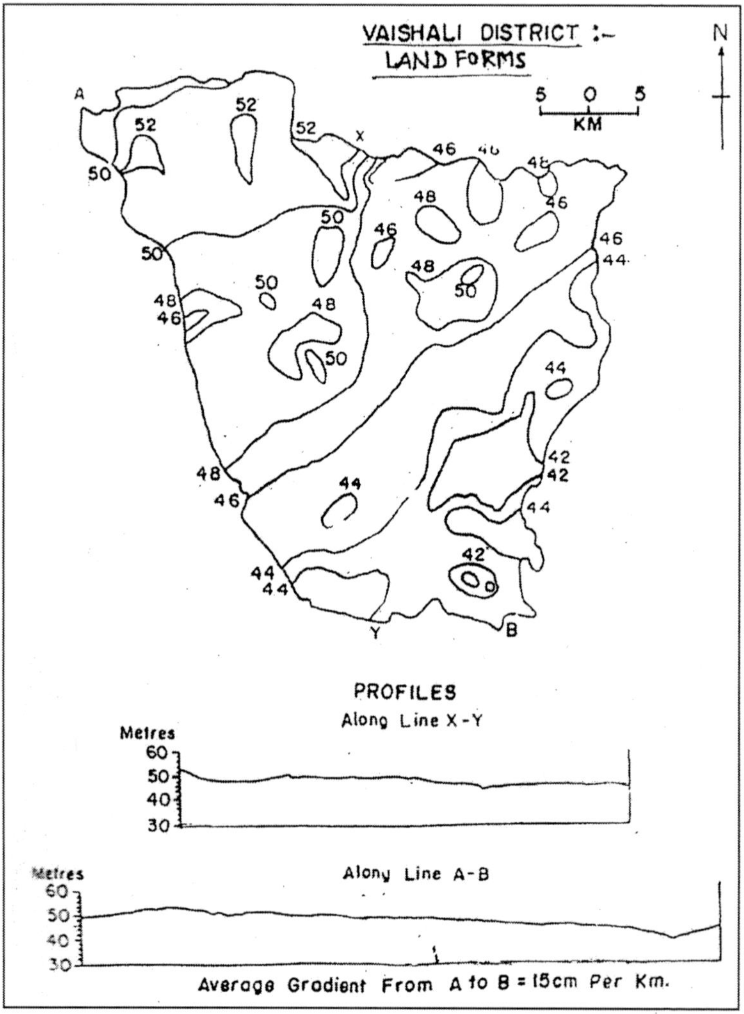
VAISHALI DISTRICT :-
LAND FORMS
N
5 0 5
KM
A
X
Y
B
PROFILES
Along Line X-Y
Metres
60
50
40
30
Along Line A-B
Metres
60
50
40
30
Average Gradient From A to B = 15cm Per Km.

Fig. 2.2

Table 2.2
Vaishali District (Land form)

Name of the anchal	Higher areas		Intermediates areas		Lower areas	
	Area in Sq. Kms.	% of anchal	Area in Sq. Kms.	% of anchal	Area in Sq. Kms.	% of anchal
1. Vaishali	126.81	100	-	-	-	-
2. Patheri Belsan	71.19	96	2.64	4.9	-	-
3. Lalganj	125.83	87	18.77	13	-	-
4. Bhagwanpur	26.02	22	92.25	78	-	-
5. Goraul	64.27	65	34.60	35	-	-
6. Chehra Kelan	47.81	70	20.49	30	-	-
7. Patepur	-	-	241.20	94	15.40	6.0
8. Mahua	14	10	126	90	-	-
9. Jandaha	-	-	108.23	72	42.08	28
10. Raja Pakar	-	-	44.58	59	30.97	41
11. Hajipur	10.98	7.0	126.82	93	-	-
12. Raghopur	-	-	90.32	40	135.48	60
13. Bidupur	-	-	107.63	94	6.87	6.0
14. Desri	-	-	10.49	21	39.49	79
15. Sahdai Bujurg	-	-	19.30	22	70.69	78
16. Mahnar	-	-	-	-	89.87	100
Total	-	29%	-	50%	0	21%

Source : Self computation based on data available from sta

The zone which lies above 48 meters can be termed as higher regions which has been denoted by the 48 meters contour. These areas constitute 29.02% of the total area of the Vaishali district. The total area under higher region is 579.15 sq. kms. It is remarkable that the total area of Vaishali anchal is under higher region only.

The intermediate region are found between 48 meters and 44 meter contours. It measures a total area 1004.03 sq. kms which accounts for 50.34% of the total area of the district. The lower region areas are below the 44 meter contour line. These areas are totally 411.92 sq. kms which account for 20.64% of the total area of the district. The Mahnar anchal has all its areas under lower region. The micro relief features of the area exhibit a very important landscape called "Chaur" locally. These land are actually depressions thus actate flood prone zones. The shapes of chaur is like that of 'Saucer'. The chaurs are filled which waters of local surface drainage and rain water. The most important chaur is known as 'Tal Baraila'.

The total area under chaur measures 70.25 sq. kms which accounts for 3.45% of the total area of the district. Of the total area under chaur 45 sq. km (54.05%) is periodically water logged and the remaining 25.33 sq. kms (35.95%) is permanently water logged. Chaurs are mostly located between the two major North-west to south-east flowing rivers of the district. It reveals that chaurs are made along rivers as rivers deposit silt during its flood period.

Another important feature of the landform is the existence of 'diara' land. This feature is the result of meandering character of mature and old rivers. The entire anchal of Raghopur is a fine example of a large 'diara' formed by the river Ganga. The southern banks of this diara land are low and gentle in slope while the northern banks are very step as well as high. The lower part of the diara is filled with deep layers of sand and are not favourable for any kind of cultivation. It is very interesting feature of diara land is that after 40 to 50 years most of its land goes into river and new diara land is created by the river. This feature is attributed to the meandering character of the rivers. Thus the continous process of the formation and destruction of diara land goes on simultaneously. This process of formation and destruction often leads to dispute and quarrel among farmers whose land are situated there.

The land form features of the district influence considerably on land utilization which shows greater inclination towards agriculture. The higher areas in the district have a lower ratio of the agricultural land. As these areas are free from annual floods, these areas are preferred for settlement. The intermediate regions are not free from flood. These areas have higher ratio of agriculture land, because the fertility of the soil is renewed every year by the flood water. The lower region of the district have lesser ratio of agricultural land use because most of the land is inundated for a long period of the year. However, the remaining areas are very fertile and are used for growing vegetables, paddy, banana etc. The per hectare yield is highest in the district.

Drainage Pattern :

The drainage pattern of the district appears to be dendritic and rivers clearly reflect the characteristics of the old and mature stage rivers. Meandering course, shifting channels, formation of levels, ox-bow lakes dead channels etc. are the notable features which are observed in the rivers of the district. During rainy season the low lying areas are filled with rain water as well as flood waters of the rivers. These low lying areas remain water logged for a considerable period of the year and the water drains out very slowly on account of the absence of marked slope.

The river Gandak forms the western boundaries of the district. It join river Ganga in the south. The river Ganga forms the southern boundary of the district. These two rivers together have a great impact on the socio-economic life of the district. There are danger of flood every year from these two rivers since both of these are their old stage, and are unable to carry forward the water they obtain from heavy melting of Ice in the Himalayas zone and the rainfall of the monsoon. Besides these river there are also other rivers which are important as they influence the landuse pattern of the district. These rivers are in spate in rainy? Season these contributes heavy water and silt to the Ganga and Gandak rivers. As a result some parts of the district is flooded during Monsoon.

The Ganga :

The river Ganga flows down in the south of the district and forms southern boundary for a distance of about 32 kms and separates it from Patna. During rainy season the volume of the water increases too much and it spreads in wider area and flood occurs on wide areas. The volume and flow the water pushes back the water of the Gandak river causing flood into the lower regions of the district. While in summer the water dries up and the width of the river remains only 1 to 1.5 kms or river flows in its valley.

The Gandak :

This river rises in the Central mountain basin of Nepal and moving onwards south it enters Bihar traversing through the districts of West Champaran, East Champaran, Muzaffarpur and Finally Vaishali to join the river Ganga from its source to confluence it runs to a distance of 100 kms approximately. It has no contributing river. For flood protection two embankments have been constructed.

(a) one along the Chhapra district side and (b) another along sides of Muzaffarpur and Vaishali district.

The Baya :

It originates from a chaur which is about 6 kms south of the village 'Sarkar Saraiya' located about 20 kms south-west of Motihari town and merges into the Ganga river about 5 kms west of Begusarai district. Its total course is about 225 kms of which 98 kms runs in Vaishali district in a meandering manner.

The Nun :

It is tributaries of the river Burhi-Gandak. It rises from a chaur in Nartar village about 20 kms north-west of Muzaffarpur district and joins the river Burhi-Gandak in Begusarai. Its total length is about 175 kms and runs a meandering course of about 15 kms in the Vaishali district. It forms the eastern boundary of the district for about 12 kms before entering the Samastipur district.

The Ghaghra :

It is purely seasonal in character which takes its course from a chaur in Muzaffarpur and fall into the river Ganga. Its directions of flow is mainly from north-west to south-east and runs to a total of 87 kms in the district.

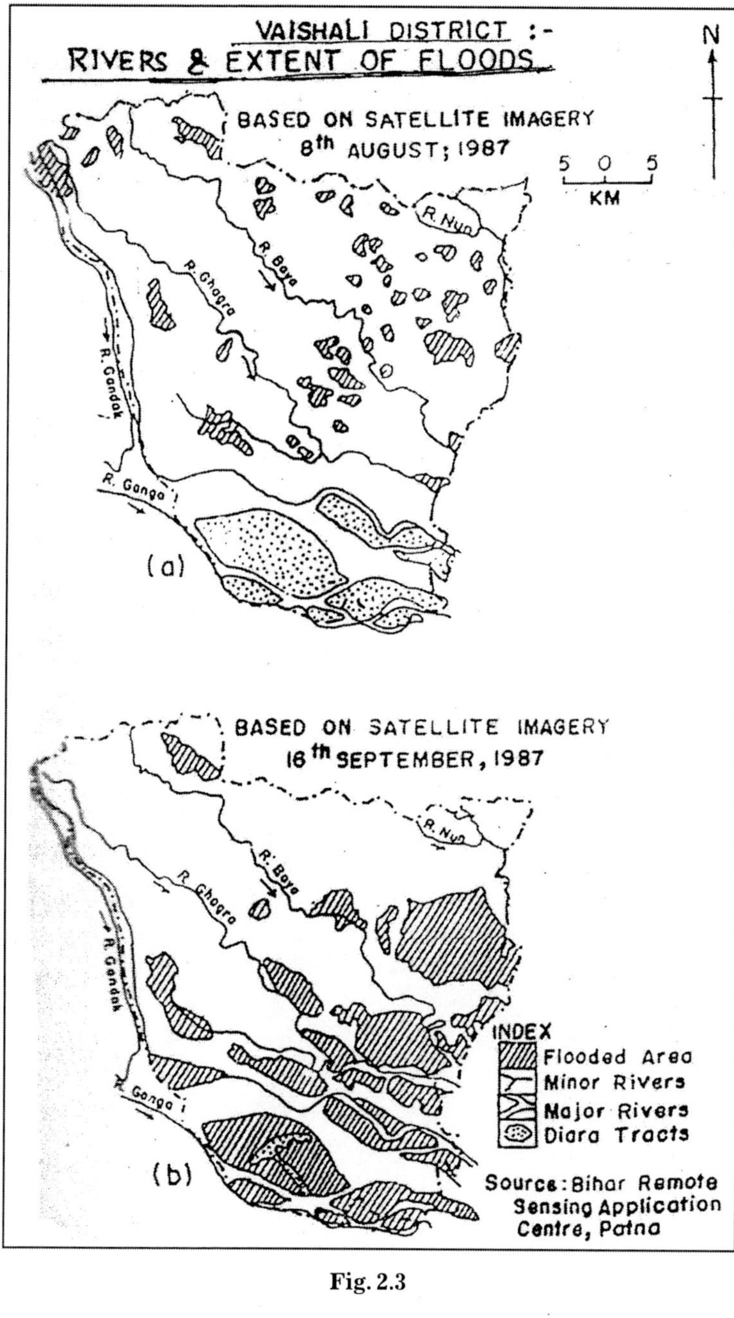
VAISHALI DISTRICT :-
RIVERS & EXTENT OF FLOODS
N
BASED ON SATELLITE IMAGERY
8th AUGUST; 1987
5 0 5
KM
R. Nun
R. Baya
R. Ghagra
R. Gandak
R. Ganga
(a)
BASED ON SATELLITE IMAGERY
16th SEPTEMBER, 1987
R. Nun
R. Baya
R. Ghagra
R. Gandak
R. Ganga
(b)
INDEX
Flooded Area
Minor Rivers
Major Rivers
Diara Tracts
Source: Bihar Remote Sensing Application Centre, Patna

Fig. 2.3

Floods :

The floods is a common phenomena in the district as rivers are in their mature stage and are unable to flow through the raised bed formed by heavy deposition of silt. The two major rivers the Ganga and the Gandak are notorius for heavy loss of properties, crops and lives during monsoon. Even smaller streams such as Nun causes flood in the eastern part of the patepur anchal. The record of collectorate of Vaishali district suggest that there were floods in the district as early as 1785.

Every year a major part of the district is inundated by the flood water. However, the intensity of the flood may differ from year to year. The table 2.3 reveals true picture of the spatial pattern of the flood prone and Non flood prone zones in different anchals of Vaishali district.

The anchal like Raghopur Sahdai-Bujurg and Mahnar have the highest ratio of floods in the district. On the other hand, the anchals of Vaishali, Mahua and Goraul have the minimum ratio (below 10%) of the flood prone area. It is to be noted that the anchal of Lalganj is entirely free from floods. The anchals of Bidupur, Patepur and Hajipur have moderate ratio.

As far as the flood free areas are concerned, the picture is entirely reversed. It means the anchals having lower ratio of flood prone areas have higher ratio of flood free areas. The drainage pattern is highly influenced by the relief, the higher tracts have lower ratio of flood while the lower tracts have higher ratio of flood.

In recent years the intensity of flood have increased considerably. The flood of 1987 can be cited to support this fact. In 1987 the whole Bihar plain was in the grip of unprecedented flood. The two maps (Fig 2a and 2b drawn with the help of the satellite imageries provided by the Bihar remote sensing application centre (BRSAC) Patna shows a clear pattern of the flood in Vaishali district in 1987. The first map is made in August month, during this month flood was in the area of 114.06 sq. kms accounting for about 5.6% of the total area. The second map is taken by the satellite on 16th September 1987. During this month the flood took a nasty lack and inundated almost 1/4th of the total area. Even in such a devastating flood the anchal of Vaishali, Lalganj and Garaul remained flood free while the anchal of Patepur, Jandaha, Sahdoi-Bujurg, Mahnar, Bidupur, Mahua and Raghopur were under the grip of severe flood. Flood could be advantegeous as well as problematic. On the one hand they maintain and restore the fertility of the soil by the deposition of fresh silts. On the other hand, they destroy standing crops, roads and settlements etc.

The impact of flood in the rainy season of 2007 (July-Sept 07) has been severe. It was highly affected the lower areas of the district, The repetation of flood has damaged lives and wealth of the district

The floods are mainly caused by blockage in the way of the drainage of Ganga heavy precipitation in catchment area and inadequate capacity of dispassed lands to hold water. Although Nowdays effective steps have been taken by the Bohar government to combat flood. These include settlement on high grounds, digging of channels etc. All that is being attempted is only to moderate the water flow resulting from rainfall by the construction of reservoirs, detention basins etc. and prevent its spill over to countryside and thus reduce the damage since human control over rainfall has not been possible.

Climate :

The study of climate forms an important part of the geographical study of a region. The climatic elements viz. temperature, rainfall, wind etc. influence to a great extent the landuse as well as agriculture and human occupation.

India is a monsoon land and climate is to a very great extent is controlled by Monsoon. The wand Monsoon owes its origin from the Arabic work "Mausim" meaning season. Monsoon is a seasonal wind which changes its direction with

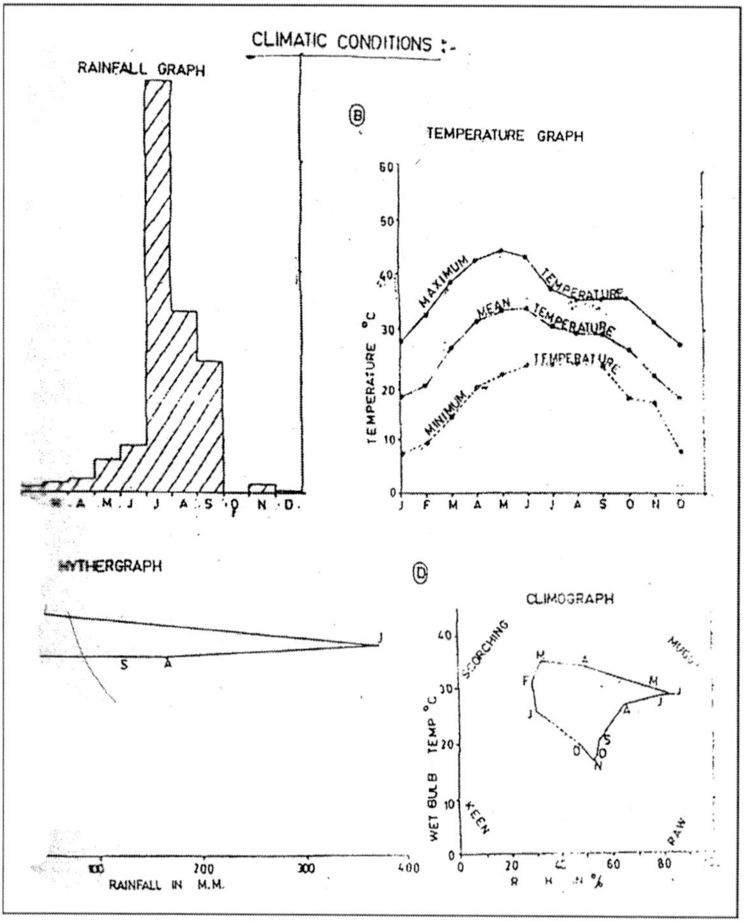
CLIMATIC CONDITIONS :-
RAINFALL GRAPH
A M J J A S O N D
B
TEMPERATURE GRAPH
MAXIMUM TEMPERATURE
MEAN TEMPERATURE
MINIMUM TEMPERATURE
TEMPERATURE °C
60
50
40
30
20
10
0
J F M A M J J A S O N D
HYTHERGRAPH
RAINFALL IN M.M.
100
200
300
400
D
CLIMOGRAPH
SCORCHING
KEEN
RAW
WET BULB TEMP °C
0
20
60
80

Fig. 2.4

the change of season. Several scholars have defined the monsoon wind. However, a precise definition of Monsoon is a matter of choice because one needs the frame with a set of rules which embraces all facets of the monsoon. Although the word 'Monsoon' was coined much later, M.V. Unakar, an Indian Scholar drew are attention nearly fifty years ago to many verses in the Rigveda which praise 'Pranjay', the God of rain and the creator of plants and living creatures.

Vaishali is a new district and about two decades ago it was a part of the old Muzaffarpur district. Thus, the temperature and rainfall etc. which were reported by the Muzaffarpur weather station have been used for the present study. There is very little difference in weather between various districts of Bihar plain.

Table 2.3
Vaishali District
(Average, Maximum and Minimum temperature and relative humidity at Muzaffarpur)

Months	Maximum temperature in °C	Minimum temperature in °C	Mean relative humidity in %
January	22.60	9.50	74
February	25.00	11.16	69
March	31.50	15.61	50
April	35.77	21.05	46
May	36.16	24.33	43
June	34.33	25.88	76
July	32.33	26.16	82
August	31.72	26.00	85
September	31.77	25.50	83
October	30. 94	21.55	76
November	27.50	14.04	74
December	23.50	9.88	77

Source : Bihar district Gazetteer, Muzaffarpur

The table 2.3 Shows the temperature and relative humidity conditions of the area. From the table we can see that the temperature begins to rise rapidly after March and reaches the maximum in the month of May. May is the hottest month of the year while January is the coldest month to the year. The rise in temperature is closely linked with the northword shift of the sun. This rising trend in checked by the arrival of Monsoon by 2°-4° in the month of June or July.

The rapid fall in temperature could be observed after the withdrawal of Monsoon in October when the Mercury drops to absolute 30°c. The advent of winter season is marked by a sharp fall of temperature about 3°c in the month of November. January is the coldest month. The mean annual range of temperature is only 14°-19°C. The average annual humidity of the area is around 71%. It varies from month to month. The lowest relative humidity (46%) can be observed in the month of April. This is due to excess dry weather condition prevailing during summer season. After the arrival of Monsoon winds the relative humidity begins to rise and reaches minimum (85%) in the month of June and September the average relative humidity remains more than (80%). The relative humidity is important as it forms cloud and precipitation in the form of dew, mist, fog, rainfall, snowfall etc.

Among the above climatic phenomena Rainfall is the most important since it is responsible agriculturals activities and cropping pattern in the area. It directly influences the landuse pattern of an areas. The earliest systematic study of rainfall data appeared in 1889. It was a valuable publication by H.Y. Blanford. The average annual rainfall in Vaishali district is around 918.5 mm. But there can be variation in rainfall anchalwise which is event in the table 2.5. The minimum rainfall in Vaishali district can be seen in Mahua anchal where it is 657.3 mm while maximum rainfall is recorded in Lalganj anchal it is 1083.77mm.

The three anchals viz. Bidupur, Patepur and Mahua recorded an annual rainfall above 1000mm and of the remaining anchals Raghopur and Vaishali have an annual rainfall between 900 and 1000mm. New anchals of

Bhagwanpur, Desri, Patheri Belsar, Raja Pakar and Chehra Kalan are also receiving annual rainfall between 800-1000mm. Hajipur and Goraul anchals receive rainfall between 600-700mm annually.

Thus a very subtle variations observed in the amount of rainfall in different sections of Vaishali district. There can be an obvious explanation for these variations. However, the variable role of the monsoon can not be accurately predicted. Monsoon clouds are dreaded for its eccentric nature which may result in the micro-level variations in the distribution of rainfall in this district.

The table 2.5 shows the mean monthly rainfall in Vaishali district. It clearly shows that the four months of June, July, August and September are highly rainy months of the year. During these months the area receives about 87.03% of the total annual rainfall. The month of August receives the maximum amount of rainfall which is 894.5 mm and the lowest amount i.e. 3.6mm is recorded in the month of December. During the four months of March, April, November, December and the mean monthly rainfall is less than 10mm.

Table 2.4
Vaishali District
(Anchal wise normal rainfall)

Name of the Anchal	Rainfall (in mm)
Hajipur	772.0
Lalganj	1083.7
Vaishali	975.7
Garual	698.1
Mahua	675.3
Pandaha	892.6
Bidupur	949.8
Raghopur	949.8
Bhagwanpur	832.3
Desri	948.2

Raja Pakar	952.3
Chehra Kalan	888.2
Patheri Belsar	821.7
Vaishali district	918.5mm

Source : Directorate of Statistics and Evaluation, Govt. of Bihar, Patna.

Table 2.5
Vaishali District
(Monthly Rainfall)

Name of Months	Mean rainfall recieved (in mm)
January	12.2
February	18.3
March	9.5
April	7.7
May	28.4
June	152.1
July	256.5
August	294.5
September	204.0
October	47.7
November	7.8
December	3.8
Annual	1042.3

Source : Directorate of Statistics and Evaluation, Govt. of Bihar, Patna.

For a Systematic study of the climatic phenomena and as well as true analysis of the climatic elements the whole year can be divided into there district seasons, characteristics of Monsoon climate. These are : (i) Cold weather or winter (ii) Hot weather, or summer (iii) warm and wet weather of rainy season.

(ii) Cold Weather or Winter :

The winter season begins from the month of October and ends in the last week of February. The seasonal changes that occur are closely linked with the apparent motion of the sun. As the sun crosses of equator after 22th September during its south ward shift the temperature starts falling gradually. The falling temperature has a profound effect on other climatic elements. The most important of them is the pressure conditions which are completely overhauled with the fall in temperature. This results in the complete reversal in temperature, clear sky and bright sunshine etc.

However, the month of October is not comfortable since sun's rays are innese and the radiation of heat from the top soil makes the weather condition very hot and humid. But during the month of November there is a sharp fall in temperature and the sky becomes very clear making the weather condition very pleasant. During this period the cool dry winds blow. These are in true sense the north-east monsoon winds. These winds are retreating after the reversal of the pressure belts from low pressure to high pressure. There is little or no rain because of the dry nature of these winds. However in the latter part of the season i.e. during January and February there is some rainfall mainly caused by the cyclone or, depressions which come through the north-east and sweep the entire Ganga basin of our century. During winter days become shorter in length because of extreme southward position of the sun and thus, the amount of insolation is greatly reduced. Sometimes very cold chillys winds sweep the area reducing the temperature to as low as 6°c-7°c. During winter about 6.7% of the total annual rainfall is received.

(ii) Hot Weather or Summer Season :

After February, in the month of March, the temperature gradually starts rising making the weather very pleasant. This is because the north-west shift of the sun. The sun rays become straight. This results in steep rise in Mercury, which in turn results in the reversal of pressure belt from high to low, leading to complete reversal in wind direction. The weather during summer is hot and dry. A typical hot and dry wind popularly known as 'Loo' sweeps areas specially during the month of April and May. The excessive summer heat results in the steep reduction in soil moisture which has its profound effect on the agricultural activities. The cultivation of crop is done chiefly on the river sides having soil moisture required for the condition of crops like Rice, Maize etc. vegetables are also grown mainly in the dry river beds and on the diara tracts with adequate amount of soil moisture.

The summer season is marked with cyclonic disturbances which are commonly known as 'Kal Baishakhi'. These cyclones are also knows as 'Norwesters' which are responsible for good amount of rainfall. These cyclone gives relief not only from acute summer heat but also provides timely rainfall for the cultivation of crops like mango and lichi. These pre-monsoon rains are also known as 'mango-showers'.

The 'Norwesters' are often accompanied by high wind velocity, thunderstorm, lightening and subsequently rainfall. There are several views regarding the origin of 'Norwesters' but it is generally believed that it originates on account of the meeting of two different types of airmasses etc. The moist airmass coming from the Bay of Bengal and the dry airmass coming from the western side. Since both these winds are quite different in their physical as well as chemical properties they do not readily mix with each other and thus, a front or low pressure which is known as a depression or cyclone is created.

The days are generally longer during the summer season as the sun is in the northern hemisphere. During nights Mercury drops considerably because of clear sky permitting radiation of heat easily. A gentle easterly, breeze results making the nights very pleasant for the people who are harasses by the day long head and the westerly hot dry winds. The summer months receive 6.14% of the total annual rainfall.

(iii)Warm and hot or Rainy season :

By the middle of June the monsoon winds responsible for bring rain arrive. The burst moon is accompanied with thunder, lightening and heavy downpore. The sky remains overcast for most part of the monsoon months. Maximum rain is brought by the black nimbus clouds which remain at lower level. The easterly winds with heavy amount of moisture blow regularly. The high temperature of the summer months drop considerably due to heavy rainfall and greater relative humidity in the air. The two months i.e. July and August receive highest rainfall in which about 80% of the total annual rainfall is received. It is to be noted here that the monsoon months do not have rainfall at regular interval. Sometimes Monsoon rains are interpreted by long breaks between their commencement in June and termination in October.

The Monsoon winds are highly irregular, untimely and inadequate. Thus the monsoon rains are highly unpredictable. Sometimes the excess rains brought by these winds are responsible for the flooding in different part of this district. However, the rainy season is important in the sense of the most important crop of paddy is grown on a large scale during this season and thus the maximum production of paddy known as Aghani or Kharif paddy is obtained. This paddy crop is also known as 'Aus paddy' which is shown in July August and harvested in November-December. The term 'Aghani' has been derived from its period of harvesting, besides paddy, other crops like maize and vegetables are also grown in this season.

In lower tracts where floods are common feature, people have raised the area artificially for habitation and settlement. The most important example can be seen in the Raghopur block which is a diara formation and where a large area is inundated during rainy season excepts the area of settlement which has been raised artificially. Thus it can be observed that climate has a great bearing on land use and agricultural pattern of the area. It determines not only the agricultural pattern but also the size and the type of the settlement etc.

Natural Vegetation :

In ancient times the district was covered with thicks forest. The population was very thin and thus man's influence on nature was eligible. But with passage of time, as the population grew, the demand of land for the purpose of Agriculture as well as settlement increased. With the result forest covered area reduced gradually to the present status. With the forest cover at present this area is famous for its intensive cultivation in which a number of crop like paddy, wheat, maize, sugarcane, vegetables etc. are grown. Since the forest was cut ruthlessly, there was no room left for the growth or wild. However, there are some variety of natural vegetation which are still found in some areas. These include Bamboo, palm, dates, mahua, bobool, sesame, papal, neem, jamun etc. These trees are used to making furnitures, doors, windows etc. Some of these are used is medicines and in some other domestic purposes. In recent time some efforts by the government has been taken towards afforestation and plantation of trees or wastelands. Plants and trees are important not only for their commercial value and domestic use but also for maintaining the ecological balance and making the environment pollution free.

The pattern of the distribution of natural vegetation shows that the low lying areas where flooding and inundation are common have mostly needs and bushes. In moist areas the most common example of reeds are saccharum spentaneum and S. Munje. In drier areas Sirka reeds are mostly found. This reed is used in thatching and making covers for houses and carts etc. Little vegetation can be seen in the fast flowing perennial streams like Ganga and Gandak. In the southern edge of Ganga, Specially in Rahopur diara some sheltered pools are found in winter. In these pools are found some algae particularly, chera and hitella, valiisnaria and other angiosperm. The area surrounding Hajipur, is famous for fruit trees which include Mango, banana, lichi and guava etc. on the boundaries of the orchards, sisum and sugarcane are mostly planted. In the famous large chaur talberella, amphibious plants are found in its shallow water. However, in the deeper zone of this chaur, a number of aquatic plants which serve as food for the duck and fowl are found. The duck and fowl migrate to this chaur in the winter season to feed on the fish also.

There are some seasonal vegetation which grow sparsely in the crop fields. But these vegetation perish quickly and turn into humus. Some weed are removed because they are harmful for the growth of the crop.

Soil :

The type of soil and their role in the production of different crops form an important part of study of land use of an area. Soil is an import resource which determines the types as well as production of crops to be grown. The importance of soil in growing crops has been recognized by man since time immemorial. Changes have been affected by man in the upper most layer of the soils through cultivation and irrigation. Soils are next to water is man's most vital natural resources. There are diversity of opinion as to what soil is and how it is formed. Most people believe soil is weathered rock but it is partially true. Soil formation is a lengthy and complex phenomena taking place due to the interaction between climate land and vegetation.

The Soil Profile :

The development of soil in any area depends upon many factors such as climate, parental material, drainage, vegetation etc. The soil of the area under study is of depositional nature or brought up by the rivers. These are called Alluvium, However, this alluvium is not uniform throughouts the district, since the constituents i.e. silt, clay sand and loam very in their proportion. The variation if the above mentioned constituents is responsible not only for the differences in texture but also in colour. Thus different type of Alluvium can be observed in the area. Broadly speaking two main types of Alluvium–clayey soil and sandy soil are found in the area, known as 'Bangar" and "Bhith" "khaddar" locally.

Clayey Soil :

These soils are found predominantly in lower swamp and chaur lands. However these can be in patches throughouts the district. These oil become very hard in dry condition because of being impervious in nature. This property is responsible for not allowing the water to enter its inner parts. However, cracks develop when these are dry. In wet condition, the assistance of high amount of clay makes the soils, very sticky. As a result, tilling becomes very difficult during rainy season. Thus the tilling of this and involves much labour making it a costly affair.

However, this soil is very important for the cultivation of paddy crop which is the most important food crop of this area. People also use this soil of building material since it is ideal for making mud walls. Locally it is known as "Matiyar". Important crops are Rice, wheat, pulses, sugarcane etc.

Sandy Soil :

As the name suggests these soils are made up of higher proportion of sand other constituents. These soils are observed on higher sites. In these areas cropping is done mainly with the help of irrigation because water does not stays over soils and goes inside through the permeable layers. Thus, the top soil is relatively dry. The cost of irrigation makes cultivation costlier. However, the tilling operations are much easier and compared to the clayey soil. Thus, the cost of tilling is lower than that of clayey soil. Wheat is the most important crop grown in this soil. In some parts the cultivation of tobacco is also done on high scale. The local name of the sandy soil is 'Belsundari' or 'Balsundhi'. The term 'Balauhi' is also used for this soil. Important crops for this soil are maize, wheat, Banana and vegetables.

Water Resources :

Water resources play an important role in the agriculture of the region, its significance to agriculture is two fold, viz. expansion of cultivated area and switching over to more intensive cultivation. Because of the uncertainty of the rainfall in the district the agriculture has been described as a gambling with Monsoon. Water resource are of two types surface water and underground water. The first source includes tanks rivers, canals, pynes, ahar and reservoirs. The underground water is tapped by wells and tubewells which have became important these days.

In the region wells and tubewells are very important. Canal irrigation is available in a very limited area and other sources are insignificant. 60.67% of the irrigated area is irrigated by wells, 37.5% by private tubewells, 1.78% by state tubewells and 0.05% by canal. Table 2 shows the sources of water for irrigation in different parts of the district. From this able it is evident that wells are the most important source of water supply except some anchals such as Hajupur, Sahdai Bujurg and Raghopur were private tubewells play most important part in irrigation. Vaishali district is very poor in canal irrigation as only Lalgand and Raja pakar anchals have this facilities. A branch of the Tirhut canal of Gandak canal system passes through Lalganj anchals. 2.11 lakh hectares of land of Vaishali district is cropped out of this only 0.85 lakh hectares is irrigated.

Thus only about 39% of the cropped area of district is irrigated. Irrigation facility may vary from place . Sahdai Bujurg is the most irrigateds anchal of the district where 52% of the cropped area is irrigated, followed by Hajipur and Goraul anchals where irrigation is available in 49% of its cropped area.

Table 2.6
Vaishali District
Source of Water supply (% of Area)

Anchal	Canal	State tubewells	Private tubewells	others
1. Vaishali	-	6.29	14.24	75.46
2. Patheri Belsan	-	2.38	24.33	69.75
3. Lalganj	0.46	-	45.38	54.26
4. Bhagwanpur	-	4.05	32.05	70.22
5. Goraul	-	-	49.83	51.17
6. Chehra Kelan	-	3.28	42.31	32.87

7. Patepur	-	-	33.85	66.15
8. Mahua	-	-	18.11	81.89
9. Jandaha	-	-	21.42	78.58
10. Raja Pakar	-	2.05	29.33	72.33
11. Hajipur	-	-	55.02	38.47
12. Raghopur	-	-	65.31	30.87
13. Bidupur	-	10.38	24.33	65.29
14. Desri	-	-	46.22	32.88
15. Sahdai Bujurg	-	-	55.41	43.80
16. Mahnar	-	-	30.24	74.10
Total	**0.05**	**1.78**	**37.50**	**60.67**

Source : Office of the District Statistics and evaluation Vaishali.

Table 2.7
Vaishali District
Crop wise irrigation 2001

Name of the Crop	Crop area in hectares	Irrigated are in hectares	Percent of the crop area
1. Paddy	6083	1643	2.70
2. Maize	25215	10153	41.93
3. Vegetables	10612	7488	70.56
4. Wheat	46992	41017	87.28
5. Barley	923	253	27.47
6. Pulses	3114	6	0.21
7. Mung	18086	36.34	20.25
8. Banana	2596	404	62.37
9. Oilseeds	1796	861	47.99
10. Jute	691	-	-
11. Marua	923	-	-

Source : Office of the District Statistics and evaluation Vaishali, Hajipur.

References :

1. Cookling, S.C. and Yeastes, M. (1976) : Man's Economic environment, p. 105.
2. Oldham, R.D. (1901) : Notes on the Geology of the Sone valley, Memoir of the Geological survey of India. Vol. XXXI, p. 1-128.
3. Dunn, J.A. (1942) : Memoir of the Geological Survey of India. Vol. XXVII. p. 1-6.

4. Narain, H. (1965) : Airborne magnetic surveys. Proceedings of Seminar on Earth Science, Part I Geophysics The Indian Geographical Union, Hyderabad.
5. Goddess, Arthur : "Alluvial Morphology of Indo-Gengetic Plain." Its mapping and Geological significance". Transactions of the institute of Geographers. p. 253-256.
6. District Gazetteer of Muzaffarpur (1958), p. 7.
7. District Gazetteer of Muzaffarpur (1958), p. 5.
8. District Gazetteer of Saran (1960), p. 2.
9. Ibid, p. 166.
10. Gupta, A.D. (1985) : Flood and Drougth control in Bihar : Present situation and future strategy, Keynote address in science for society, Patna Science College, Special Publication p. 1-7.
11. Jaknada, A.D. (1972) : Flood controls measures in India, Control water and power commission report.
12. Spate, O.H.K and Learwonth, A.T.A (1967) : India and Pakistan, p. 46.
13. An historical account of the trade winds and Monsoon observable in the seas between and near the tropics with on attempt to assign the physical cause of said winds (1986) : Phil. Trans : Royal Society London, 26. pp. 153-168.
14. P.K. Das (1998) : The Monsoon, National Book Trust of India, p. 5.
15. Correlation between Pre Monsoon conditions over N.W. India and subsequent Monsoon rainfall over N.W. India and the Peninsula. Indian Meteorological deptt. Science note Vol. No. 6 (1928).
16. Blanford, H.P. (1989) : Climates and weather of India, Ceylone and Burma, Mcmillan company, New York.
17. Clarke, K.G.T. (1932) : The vicissitudes of the summer rainfall of the Indo-Gangetic plain and the Assam valley, vol. XVII. Ne-98, p. 186-87.
18. District Gazetteers of Muzaffarpur (1958), p. 7-10.
19. Bunting Brain, J. (1965-66) : The Geography of Soil. p. 19.
20. Trenchar, M. and Adlar, R. (1960) : The soil and its fertility, p.1
21. Dayal, P. (1953) : Bihar in Maps, Kusum Publication, Patna, p. 136.

3

Demographic Features

Land resources has been the basic tool of civilization. Man has used land for shelters and growing foodgrains. As such settlements have grown in large numbers in the form of villages, towns, cities etc. Hence, man is the basic user of land and in that process human being used the land to a great extent. On the other land, landforms have influenced growth of population, agricultural pattern, settlements occupation etc.

The geographical phenomena both physical and human are in a state of constant and any complete study must take this fact into consideration. The ability as well as the efficiency of man are always changing with the change in ecological structure. The efficiency and ability of man are governed by a number of factors which includes location, environmental conditions Political condition, climate etc. The study of human resources has now attained great importance as landuse and changes being brought about in its use depend chiefly on the nature of the human resources which includes mainly qualitative and the quantitative aspects. "It is man, who tries to obtain his objectives by exercising human control on land resources."

As already started the quantitative aspect of human resources consists of the growth size, density, age and sex structure, occupational structure etc. on the other hand, the qualitative aspect includes traits, ability, skills, technical know how, health and hygiene etc. Thus, the study of human resources is a part of the social geography.

The present area under study–Vaishali district being a part of the month Bihar plain is one of the densely settled regions of the state of Bihar. At the same time, this region is also the part of the densely settled region of middle Gangetic plain. The rich fertile alluvium with enough rain provided by the S.W. Monsoon has provided greater opportunities for man to adopt agriculture as their main occupation.

According to 2011 Census total population of the district is 3495021 while the 2001 census shows a total population is 2712389 in this district. Considering its small size the district definitely has large population. In contrast to various south-east Asian countries type of agriculture being practiced in this region is purely subsistence with the number of people swelling every year. The situation is thus definitely alarming until any substantial progress in the nature of cropping takes place leading to greater productivity.

The steep rise in population is putting on extra pressure on the existing land resources and as such as the face of the land is being greatly affected by its unplanned use. The

Source : https://media.nationalgeographic.org/assets/photos/000/249/24969.jpg

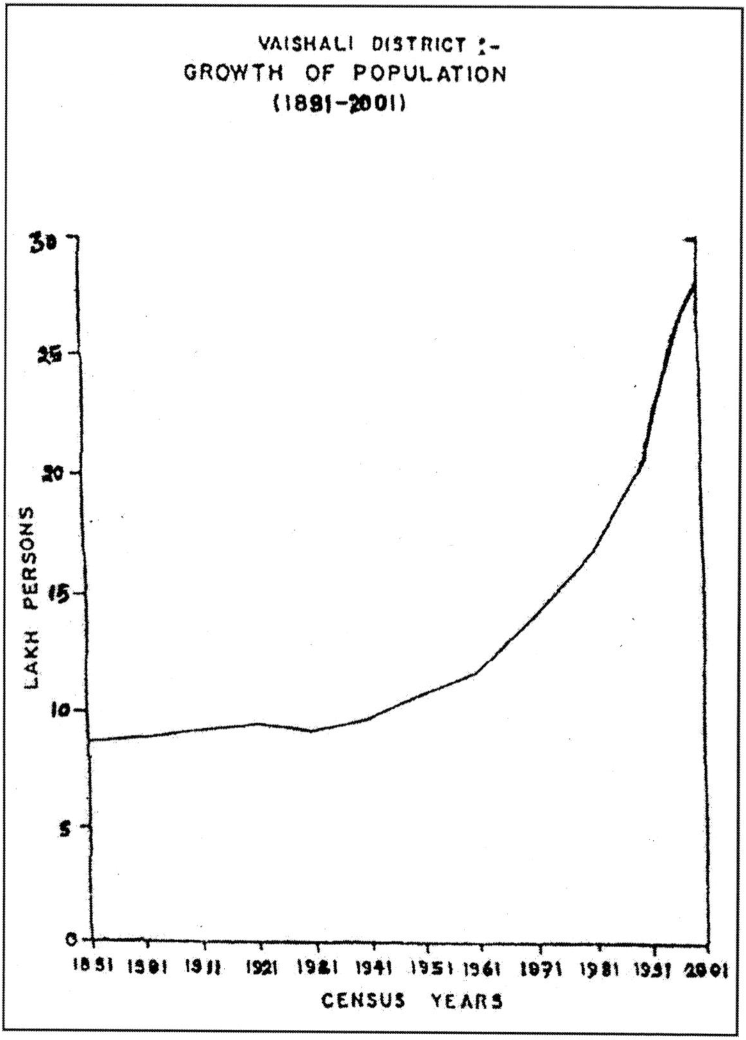
VAISHALI DISTRICT :-
GROWTH OF POPULATION
(1891-2001)
LAKH PERSONS
30
25
20
15
10
5
0
1891 1901 1911 1921 1931 1941 1951 1961 1971 1981 1991 2001
CENSUS YEARS

Fig. 3.1

population is rising without any alternative source of livelihood, thus it has resulted into intense crowding and pressure on land and natural resources." The overcrowding in this region therefore, is "bound to hamper economic development and ultimately bring in its wake a definite lowering in the standards of living."

Growth of Population :

Trend of population growth of any region does not remain static. It is bound to change every moment. The changes which takes place in the number of people in a certain period of time is called growth of population.

The population growth is caused by two factors :

(i) The fertility and mortality rates

(ii) Mobility of the population

The growth caused by the fertility and mortality rates is known as Natural growths which is by and large solely responsible for the changes in the number of people. This growth is either positive or negative. In normal condition fertility rate is always higher than the mortality rate and thus a positive growths recorded. The second factor population mobility is to some extent responsible for population growth. This mobility is caused by "Push and Pull" factors. If the push factor is greater than the pull factors, people will tend to migrate outside the region but when the pull factor is greater then push factor, the people with be attracted the region. Thus, the growth of population is a continuous process and is caused by the factors discussed above.

As the historical records reveal Vaishali district has remained inhabited since the prehistoric era but it is almost impossible to tell the exact population at that times. However, since 1872 when the first census took place, data regarding the number of people is available. Although the techniques adopted in that census were crude but there is no denying the fact that it was the beginning of an effort towards collecting demographic information.

Till 1971 the population figures have been taken from district census of Muzaffarpur district of which the present Vaishali district was a part in the form of Hajipurs subdivision. However, since 1981, the district census handbook of the present Vaishali District has been consulted. The census figure for the area under study are not available for the period prior to 1951. Thus, the trend of growths for the whole of Muzaffarpur district has been accepted for the Vaishali district as well. The table 5.1 shows that there has been an all thorough positives growth of population during the period 1881-1991 except for the decade 1911-21 which shows a negative growth of 3.18%. This happened on account of excess deaths from Epidemic of plague, cholera and malaria which were spread in different part of the country.

The state of Bihar as a whole registered a decline of 0.66% during that period. After this period when epidemic was controlled rapid growth of population began and during the next two decades the growth recorded were 6.75% and 10.32% respectively. The rate of percentage varied due to other natural calamities like flood, drought and resultant famines.

Table 3.1
Vaishali District
Decadal growth of population

Years	Population	% Variation in the Total Population		
		Vaishali district	Bihar	India
1891	691916	-	-	41.93
1891	726581	5.01	5.94	-
1901	737343	1.55	0.22	-
1911	761749	3.24	3.67	5.76
1921	737525	-3.18	-0.66	-0.31
1931	787308	6.75	11.45	11.05
1941	868558	10.32	12.20	14.22
1951	942472	8.51	10.27	13.31
1961	1133086	20.32	19.77	21.50
1971	1347990	19.05	21.44	24.80
1981	1662527	23.24	24.06	25.00

1991	2146065	29.08	23.49	23.50
2001	2718442	26.38	28.43	23.00
2011	3495021	28.63	25.40	17.64

Source : District Census Handbook Vaishali 1981 and Muzaffarpur 1961 and 1971, 1991 and 2001; census office, Patna.

The decade of 1891-1901 shows on exceptionally low increase in the population of only 1.55% in the district. This can be attributed to four factors which are (i) The famine of 1897 (ii) substantial reduction in birth rate (iii) plague epidemic (iv) emigration.

However, there has been a much faster growth after 1951 as the last four decades 1951-61, 1961-71, 1971-81 and 1981-91 have registered the percentage increase of 20.22%, 19.05%, 23.24% and 29.08% respectively. The faster growth rater after 1951 has been on account of the following factors (i) Provision of Medical care (ii) Increase in overall facilities for the farmers (iii) Improvement in agricultural techniques (iv) Infrastructural developments including Hospitals, schools, roads, water supplies etc.

Variation in Population :

Upto now an analysis of the growth of population in different decades for the vaishali district taken as one unit has been done. This analysis gives picture of he growth of population of the district as a whole. However, the situation may not be the same in different parts of the district for various other reasons which requires specific investigation.

Table 3.2
Vaishali District
Changing Anchalwise growth of population

	Percent Growth of Population					
Name of Anchals	**1951-61**	**1961-71**	**1971-81**	**1981-91**	**1991-2001**	**2001-2011**
Hajipur	24.12	25.06	32.24	32.56	28.22	26.96
Lalganj	17.32	28.95	22.59	27.87	21.03	30.26
Vaishali	17.92	8.24	21.07	28.34	26.32	28.10

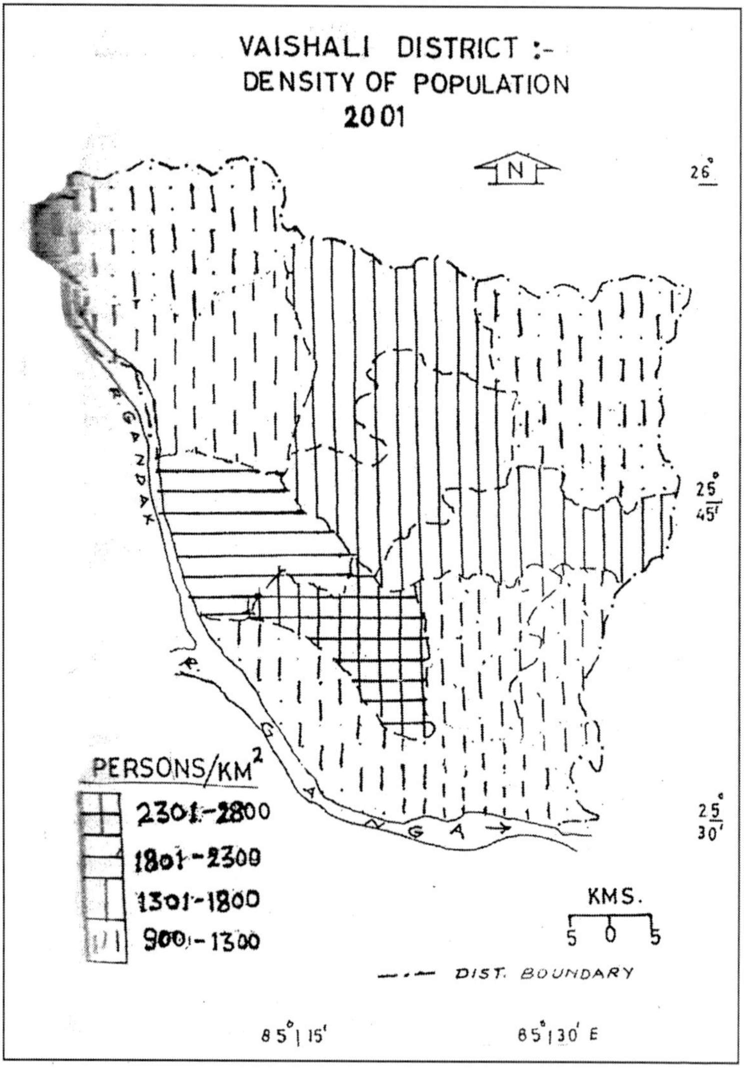
VAISHALI DISTRICT :-
DENSITY OF POPULATION
2001
N
26°
25°
45'
25°
30'
R. GANDAK
R. GANGA
PERSONS/KM²
2301-2800
1801-2300
1301-1800
900-1300
KMS.
5 0 5
DIST. BOUNDARY
85° 15'
85° 30' E

Fig. 3.2

Goraul	19.63	20.57	19.39	28.24	23.35	31.06
Mahua	19.63	20.28	24.99	29.36	28.23	30.31
Patepur	18.37	19.80	22.63	33.71	30.07	30.88
Jandaha	19.63	20.28	24.99	29.36	28.23	32.90
Paterhi Belsar	-	-	-	-	21.39	28.48
Mahnar	19.24	21.04	24.39	23.81	22.20	25.20
Sahdai Bujurg	21.10	14.94	18.76	27.22	21.43	28.09
Bidupur	20.18	21.56	28.53	26.80	25.46	29.62
Raghopur	27.81	4.83	15.79	00.12	02.33	29.07
Rajapakar	-	-	-	-	29.35	31.53
Desri	-	-	-	-	22.50	12.69
Chehra Kalan	-	-	-	-	26.20	29.93
Bhagwanpur	-	-	-	-	19.21	28.08
Vaishali	20.00	19.05	23.24	29.08	26.38	28.63

Source : District Census Handbook Muzaffarpur 1961 and 1971 and Vaishali 1981, 1991, 2001 and 2011; census office, Patna.

According to table 3.2 the percent growth of population in various anchals of Vaishali district since 1951 the highest growth (29.08%) has been recorded during the decade 1981-91. The table clearly shows that the population growth rate has been increasing since 1951. The growth rate has increased substantially since 1971. Prior to 1971 it was 19.05% during 1961-71 which rose to 23.24% during 1971-81. It rose at a much faster rate during 1981-91 when the growth rate was recorded at 29.08%.

During 1951-61 there has been an altogether positive growth rate of above 17% in all the anchals of the district. Three anchals viz. Raghopur (27.91%), Hajipur (24.12%) and Sahdai Bujurg (21.10%) recorded a maximum growth rate more than the average for the district (20.22%) as a whole. The minimum growth rate of 17.32% was recorded in Lalganj anchal.

The next decade of 1961-71 shows on interesting situation. Lalganj where the growth of rate was minimum during 1951-61 registered the highest growth rate of 28.95% during 1961-71 recorded the minimum growth rate of 4.83% during 1961-71. Thus the entire picture of growth rate seems to have been inverted during this decade. Seven anchals viz. Lalganj (28.95%), Goraul (20.57%), Hajipur (26.06%), Mahua

(20.28%), Patepur (19.08%), Mahnar (21.04%) and Bidupur (21.56%) recorded a greater growth than the district average (19.05%)

This inverted picture may be on account of temporary migrations of Agricultural labourers which take place generally in rural areas in search of labour earnings. However, other factors like steep rise in birth rate may not be ruled out. The rate of growth in general increased towards a greater maxima.

The next decade of 1971-81 shows an increase again the maximum growth rate. The maximum growth rate recorded in 1961-71 was 28.95% in Lalganj anchal which rose to 32.24% in Hajipur anchal during 1971-81. The minimum growth rate of 15.79% was recorded in Raghopur anchal four anchals viz. Hajipur (32.24%), Bidupur (28.53%), Mahua (24.99%), and Mahnar (24.39%) recorded a greater growth rate than the district average of 23.24%.

The last decade of 1981-91 has again witnessed a rise in the maximum growth rate of 32.24% in Hajipur which was recorded during 1971-81. It now reached to 33.71 in Patepur. Four anchals namely Patepur (33.17%), Hajipur (32.50%), Mahua (29.36%), and Jandaha (29.29%) recorded a greater growth rate than the district average of 29.08%. The minimum growth rate of only 0.12% has been reached in Raghopur anchal. It is interesting to observe that Raghopur has witnessed an abnormal pattern of growth rate doing the last four decades (Table 5.2). There has been a sudden fall during 1961-71 and a sudden rise during 1971-81 and again a sudden fall during 1981-91 has been witnessed. This situation is on account of its being a diara tract of the river Ganga. The unstable situation in agriculture as well as in social life caused by instability of flooding. The flood, sometimes result into large scale temporary migration of people to adjoining areas causing steep fall in population. However when the condition becomes favourable people start converging again tot he same region from where they have fields During the decade of 1991-2001 the district had a growth rate of 26.38%.

Seven anchals of district have shown growth rate of more than 25%. Lowest growth rate observed is Raghopur anchal (2.33) and highest growth rate is in Patepur (30%).

Pressure of man on land :

According to 2001 census the total population of Vaishali district is 2712389 out of which 2531734 persons are rural and the rest 180655 person are urban. In order words 93.33% of the total population is rural and the rest 6.66% is urban. The urban population is concentrated in the three urban centres of Hajipur, Lalganj and Mahnar anchals. The largest urban centre is Hajipur town, located in Hajipur anchal. It constitutes about 64% of the total urban population of the district. The man-land ration in Vaishali district in 2001 census comes to 1332 persons per sq. kms.

Table 3.3
Vaishali District
Changing population density

Name of Anchals		1971	1981	1991	2001	2011
Hajipur	Urban	967	1279	1850	2552	2158
	Rural	800	1006	1290		
Lalganj	Urban	709	869	1135	1419	1590
	Rural	663	691	1040		
Vaishali		570	687	896	1154	1479
Goraul		718	876	1121	1371	1796
Mahua		768	969	1227	1559	2031
Patepur		541	564	887	1104	1443
Jandaha		724	861	1157	1385	1837
Paterhi Belsar		-	-	-	-	
Mahnar	Urban	792	986	1180	1403	1469
	Rural	658	810	1014		
Sahdai Bujurg		548	769	995	1134	1354
Bidupur		893	1148	1441	1811	2347
Raghopur		331	453	493	831	1031
Rahapakar		-	-	-	1592	2093
Desri		-	-	-	1555	2005

Chehra Kalan	-	-	-	1482	1918
Bhagwanpur	-	-	-	1374	1757
Vaishali	649	794	1054	1332	1479
Bihar	324	402	497	880	1106
India	173	208	267	324	382

Source : District Census Handbook Muzaffarpur and Vaishali 1971, 1981, 1991 and 2001; census office, Patna.

Index of Change :

The table 5.3 gives an account of the variation in density in population for the last three beginning from 1971. In 2001 figures shows that the average density of population of Vaishali district is 1332 person per sq. kms. The corresponding figures for Bihar and India are 880 and 324 respectively. In 1971 the average density of population of the Vaishali district was 663 person per sq. kms. Which cleanly indicates that it has almost doubled during the last 30 years. The average density for Bihar in 1971 was 324 persons/sq. kms which rose to 880 in the year 2001, which shows almost the same pattern as observed in Vaishali district. The average density for India in 1971 was only 173 persons/sq.km which increased to 324 persons/sq.kms in 2001. it is also on the same pattern as the Vaishali district and Bihar state as a show. However the situation in different anchals of the district is not the same. The table 3.3 shows that the density of population has been increasing at a fast rate in almost all the anchals of Vaishali district since 1971. In 1971 seven anchals of Vaishali district namely Hajipur, Lalganj, Goraul, Mahua, Jandaha, Mahnar and Bidupur recorded a higher density that the district average. The highest density (967/Sq.kms) was recorded at Hajipur anchal and the lowest (331/sq.km) was registered at Raghopur. In 1981 maximum population density (1278/sq.km) was once again observed in Hajipur anchal. The total number of anchals having higher density that the district total average remained at seven and thus the pattern of density did not change in 1981.

However, the maximum and the minimum value attained greater heights, which indicates a much faster increase in populations. In 1991, the pattern of the distribution of density again remained the same, but the maximum density of Hajipur rose to a much greater height to 1850/sq. kms which is approximately very close to density figures of 497 persons/ sq. kms observed for Bihar state in 1991. Once again the same anchal as in the case of previous census year of 1971 and 1981 registered a higher density than the district average of 1054 persons/sq.kms.

Hajipur is the district headquarter of Vaishali district and is also situated in close proximity of state capital Patna. Industries related to manufacture of electronic components, Agrobased products, sugar mills are going to be setup at Hajipur. Thus, it is being highly influenced by the vicinity of Patna district. Hence it is bound to witness a greater spurt of population in near future.

Distribution of Population :

The spatial pattern of distribution of population in 2001 shows that the Northern part of the district has a greater share of the total population of the area. The southern as well as the south-eastern parts have relatively lower share of the population of the district. This difference has been caused chiefly by physical, social and locational factors. A more scientific study of the distribution of population can be done by taking into account of the three elements viz. percent of total area of the district in each anchal and the percent of population of the district in each anchal and the density of population in each anchal. A correlative among the above elements would reveal the correct pictures of the distribution of population. The total area of the district can be divided into four grades of population density which are :

(i) 800-1300 persons sq.km.

(ii) 1301-1800 persons sq. kms

(iii) 1801-2300 persons sq.km.

(iv) 2301-2800 persons sq.km.

The first category of population density includes the

anchals of Raghopur Vaishali, Patheri Belsar, Patepur, Sahdai Bujurg of the district. It has a share of 37.85% of the total area of the district and has 29.13% of the total population (Table 5.4). The minimum concentration in Raghopur is purely on account of negative physical factors like excess flooding by the river Ganga on account of being a diara tract, poor soil condition and poor accessibility. The next category of population density i.e. 1201-1600 includes a considerable part of the district.

Table 3.4
Vaishali District
Distribution of population

Name of the Anchal	Percent of total area of the district	Percent of total population of the district	Density of population
Vaishali	6.22	5.39	1154
Patheri Belsar	3.64	2.74	1076
Lalganj	7.43	7.51	1419
Bhagwanpur	5.80	5.98	1374
Goraul	4.85	4.99	1371
Chehra Kalan	3.35	3.71	1482
Patepur	12.60	10.42	1104
Mahua	6.87	8.04	1559
Jandaha	7.38	7.66	1385
Rajapakar	3.71	4.43	1592
Hajipur	7.70	12.89	2552
Raghopur	11.09	6.92	831
Bidupur	5.62	7.64	1811
Desri	2.45	2.86	1555
Sahdai Bujurg	4.30	3.66	1134
Mahnar	4.90	5.31	1403

Source : Self computation based on figures available from census office 2001; census office, Patna.

It comprises of Nine anchals viz. Lalganj, Bhagwanpur, Goraul Chehra kalan, Mahua, Jandaha, Rajapakar, Desri and Mahnar. These together account for 46.74% of the total area of the district and contains 50.49% of the total population. Thus this category has a greater uniformities in respect of

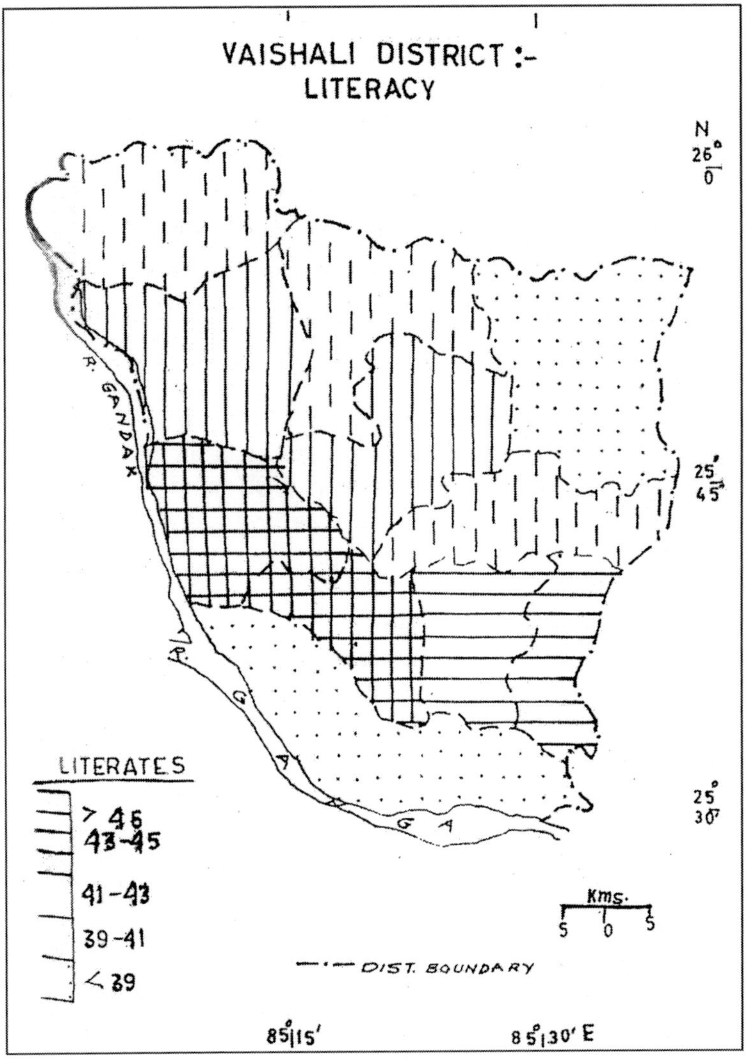
VAISHALI DISTRICT :-
LITERACY
N
26°
0'
25°
45'
25°
30'
R. GANDAK
R. GANGA
LITERATES
> 46
43-45
41-43
39-41
< 39
Kms.
5 0 5
DIST. BOUNDARY
85°15'
85°30' E

Fig. 3.3

the share of area and population.

The third category of density 1801-2300 persons per sq.km consists of only one anchal of Bidupur. This anchal has 5.62 percent of the total area of the district and contains 7.62 percent of the total population of the district. The fourth category of the population density 2301-2800 has only one anchal of Hajipur, which has a share of 7.70 percent of the total area of the district and 12.89 percent of the total population. This high density of Hajipur could be attributed to its being urban area since long, all government offices, Railways stations and zonal office of East-Central Railway are situated here. It has became nearest city from to the capital Patna and now it is to be included in the greater Patna project.

Thus it is observed that near about 75% of the total area of the district has a population density of more than 1999 person/sq.km. Therefore, this zone may be regarded as the most thickly populated area of the state.

Literacy :

According to 2001 census total literacy of Vaishalis district is 50.49%. Total literate people are (1107242) out of which 100386 people are urban while 1006856 belong to rurals areas. Hajipur is the most literate Anchals of Vaishali district with 50.16% literacy. While the literacy rate of Bihar is 47.53 and India is 64.8% respectively. Vaishali has 48.93% male literacy while 32.01% of the total female population is literate.

Occupational Structure :

The occupational of any region reveals the true picture of the utilizations of human resource. It brings out the hidden aspects of the socio-economic status of any regions and thus help in the proper planning for the managements of human resource. The census figures indicates two broad categories of workers which are main workers and marginal workers. Work has been defined as participation in any economically productive activity. Work involves not only

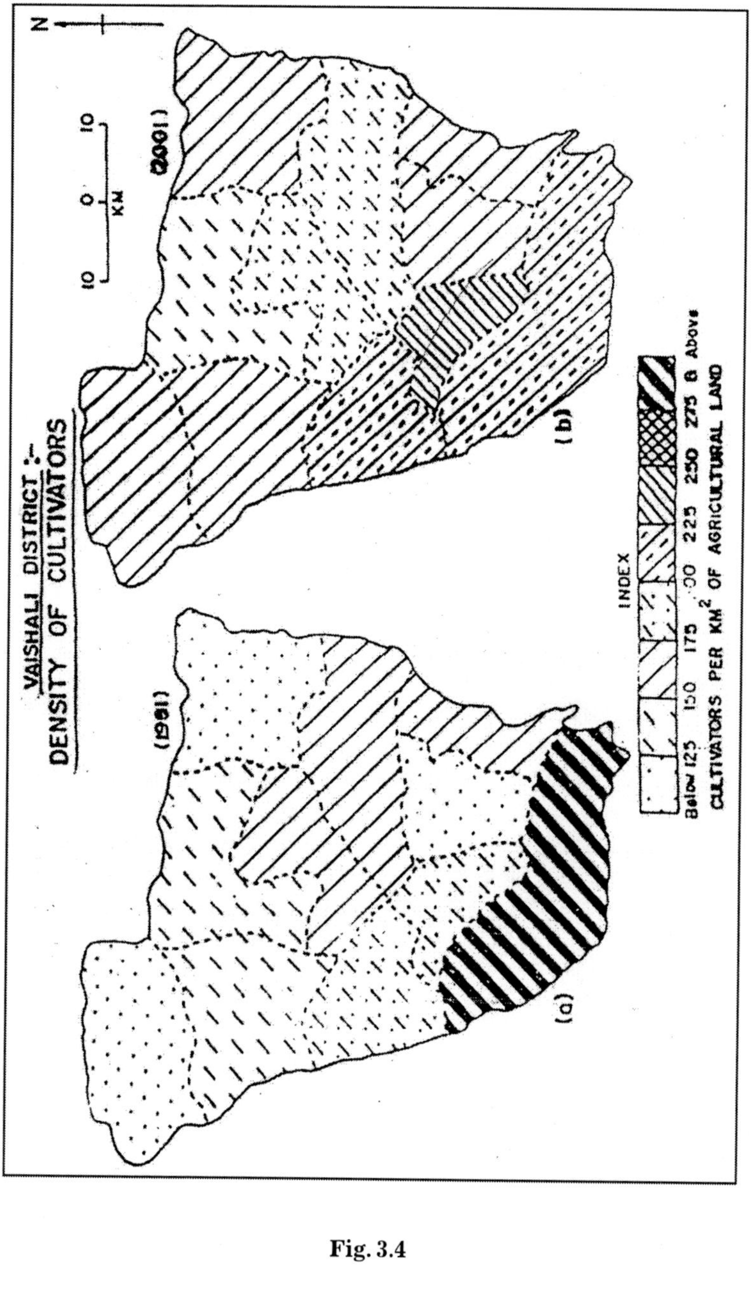
VAISHALI DISTRICT :-
DENSITY OF CULTIVATORS
N
10 0 10
KM
(1981)
(2001)
(a)
(b)
INDEX
Below 125 150 175 200 225 250 275 & Above
CULTIVATORS PER KM² OF AGRICULTURAL LAND

Fig. 3.4

actual work but also effective supervision and direction of work. It also includes unpaid work on farm or in family enterprise. A person will be called a worker. If a person works for 183 days or more in a year, he has to be treated as main worker and if a person worked for less than 183 days or 6 months in a year, he is to be treated as marginal worker.

The main workers have been further subdivided into four broad categories : (i) cultivators (ii) Agricultural labour (iii) workers engaged in manufacturing, processing, servicing in household industries, (iv) other workers : all service class, political workers artists, social workers, mining, transport workers etc.

The number of total workers in Vaishali district according to 2001 census is 769451 which also includes Marginal workers. Its share in the total population of the district is little more than 28.36%. The corresponding figure for Bihar and India are 29.13% and 37.5% respectively. Of the total workers a considerable ratio is under cultivators and agricultural labourers. It is around 83% of the total workers of the district.

In Bihar and India as a whole the cultivators and agricultural workers constitute 80.63% and 64.90% of the total working force respectively. In this way it is observed that the main component of the working is related to agricultural activities since the whole of Vaishali is purely on agricultural region producing varieties of food and non-food crops. However, as already observed production of food grain is of utmost importance.

Cultivators. :

The working force is more or less uniformly distributed over the region. It varies from 18.23% in Hajipur to 35.30% in Mahnar. Cultivators have the highest share of the working force of the region. It comes to about 27.56% of the total population in the district. The pattern of its distribution reveals a greater degree of variation in the district. It varies from 6.20% in Hajipur to 20.11 in Mahnar anchal. Fourteen

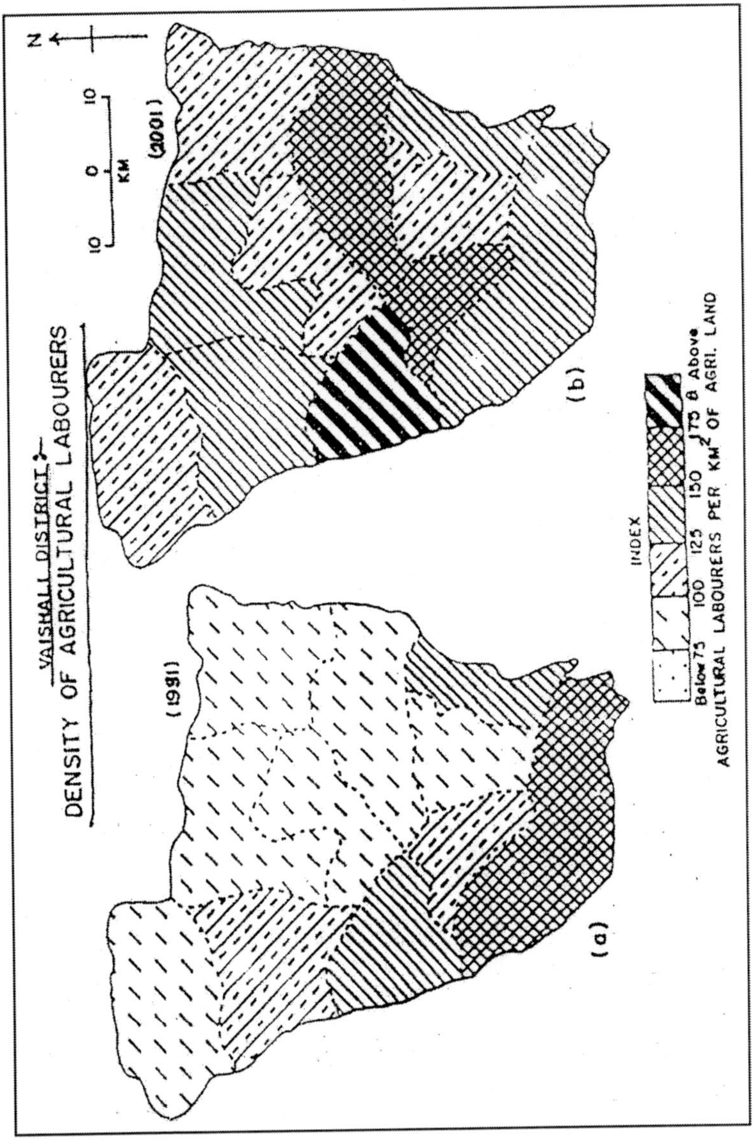
VAISHALI DISTRICT :-
DENSITY OF AGRICULTURAL LABOURERS
(1991)
(2001)
10 0 10
KM
N
(a)
(b)
INDEX
Below 75 100 125 150 175 & Above
AGRICULTURAL LABOURERS PER KM² OF AGRI. LAND

Fig. 3.5

anchals have higher ratio of cultivators than the districts average, except Hajipur and Lalaganj anchals.

It clearly indicates that the land is being owned by a large number of people in this district.

Agricultural Labourers :

The agricultural labourers from the next dominant group of the working force. It accounts for 8.12% of the total population of Vaishali district. However, it varies from 5.96% in Hajipur to 12.22% in Lalganj anchal of the district. The third group of other workers which include workers engaged in household industries and Marginal workers constitute 6.22% of the total population the region. Hajipur is the most prominent anchal having highest percentage of other workers because of its being urban centre and headquarter of Vaishali district.

Table 3.4
Vaishali District
Working Force 2001
(Figures as percent to total population)

Name of the Anchal	Total Workers	Cultivators	Agricultural labourers	Other Workers
Vaishali	21.29	10.69	6.07	2.53
Patheri Belsar	30.59	16.20	10.21	4.18
Lalganj	33.38	13.11	12.22	8.05
Bhagwanpur	28.25	15.29	6.86	6.10
Goraul	30.10	18.22	7.36	4.52
Chehra Kalan	29.89	14.51	9.02	6.36
Patepur	30.38	16.22	10.11	4.05
Mahua	23.78	12.84	7.28	3.66
Jandaha	24.48	14.23	8.17	2.08
Rajapakar	28.30	16.07	6.21	6.02
Hajipur	18.23	6.20	3.96	8.07
Raghopur	29.96	18.26	7.87	3.83
Bidupur	26.30	14.30	6.28	5.72
Desri	26.70	12.88	8.84	4.98
Sahdari Bujurg	27.41	13.78	6.87	6.76
Mahnar	35.30	20.11	9.06	6.13

Vaishali	26.87	12.53	8.12	6.22
Bihar	32.56	12.90	11.05	4.61
India	37.64	13.22	8.92	15.50

Source : Based on self computation from figures available in census 2001 at census office, Patna.

Agricultural labourers have increased 2.5 times in two decades 1980-91, 1991-2001. The third group of workers which include marginal workers and the workers engaged in manufacturing, household industries have also doubled. The maximum increase in the number of agricultural labourers is a pointer towards growing poverty on account of high rate of population growth resulting into landlessness and unemployment etc. On the other hand, the growth rate of cultivators is negligible. It was 46.45% in 1991 which fell to 38.33% in 2001. This indicates that other categories are increasing at a faster rate. Most of the villages are leaving their villages to work in urban areas as labourers in factories, houses and various services.

Dependent population :

According to 2001 census the total non working population in the district was 20,33,191 persons which is about 83.13% of the total population. The dependent or Non-working population mostly includes the old age persons, women and childrens. This dependency rate has been increasing for the last three decades. This is also result of heavy population increase and limited employment opportunity. This dependency can be reduced by giving employment in agricultural sector and also by establishing village cottage industries several schemes like 'Integrated Rural Development Programme' (IRDP) 'Jawahar Rojgar Yojna' (JRY) etc but high dependency ration clearly points towards the fact that these measures have not met with desired success. So far as the spatial pattern of the distribution of dependent population is concerned, it shows by and large uniform pattern. In almost all the anchals of the district the ration is around 74-75%

High degree of dependent population indicates the wastage of human energy which can be suitably utilized for on overall economic development. Dependency on land can be reduced by utilizing this vast human energy in sectors other than agriculture.

References :

1. Dickens Samuel, N. and Pith Forrest, R. (1963) Introduction to Human Geography, p. 12.
2. Vink, A.P.A. (1975) : Land use in advancing Agriculture, Newyork, p. 145.
3. Stamp, L.D. (1952) : Land for tomorrow, The undeveloped world.
4. Kuriyan, George (1971) : Population and Food in India, A Geographical Analysis, Studies in Applied and regional geography, Aligarh, p. 143.
5. Singh, Jasbir : Agriculture geography, Tata Mcgraw Hill publishing company Ltd. 1984, p. 135.
6. Ibid, p. 133
7. Census of Bihar.
8. Census of India.
9. Trewartha, G.T. : "A case of population Geography" Annals of the Association of American Geographers No. XLVII, 1953, pp. 71-97.
10. Ibid, p. 5.

4

Classification of Land

Landuse in an area is the cumulative outcome of historical growth, the interaction of economic forces with the natural environment and the value of society. The study of landuse has attained greater significance in the present age of scientific development and rapidly growing population. Inspite of the fact that scientific development has achieved sky limit, It has not been possible for the mankind to lesson its dependency on land. Thus land is still an invaluable resource which is inextensible as well. There has been a constant struggle always going for the best and maximum use of land to derive maximum benefit.

In a developing country like India where population is rising fastly, the study of land utilization becomes of utmost importance, so that the problem of feeding as well as providing land for their best use may be diagnosed in right prospective. The present area under study Vaishali district is a part of the middle Ganga Basin of India. This area is famous for a variety of crops.

Land Classification :

For the purpose of study and better understanding the land, It has been divided into Nine major categories of use by the Economic and Statistical Advisor Ministry of Food and Agriculture Government of India. There are : (i) Forest (ii) Barren and Uncultivated waster land, (iii) Land put to non agricultural use, (iv) cultivable wasteland, (v) Permanent pastures and others grazing land (vi) Miscellaneous tree crops, groves and rochards, (vii) other fallow land excluding current fallow (viii) current fallow (ix) Net sown area.

In Vaishali district which is a part of the depositional

land of middle Ganga plain, the land is almost flat and leveled with thick fertile alluvium. The area has a number of slow and sluggish streams joining either river Ganga or its tributaries. The climate is warm and humid. With these physical characteristics landuse of the area is dominated by foodcrops like rice, wheat, maize etc. The agriculture is substance sedentary and therefore, land is being used mostly for the purpose of growing grains for earning the livelihood.

Thus, the pattern is entirely different from what we find in the British and American landuse. It means that the, principle of landuse that have evolved from the middle latitude experience can not be applied directly to tropics because the socio-economic conditions in this area is very different from the mid-latitude regions. The major landuse types of Vaishali districts can be broadly put into two major groups (i) Arable lands (ii) Non Arable lands which are discussed separately in the following paragraphs.

Arable Lands :

There are 62.30% about area of the district is under new sown area . It fallow lands are added to this area it becomes about 70% of the total area of the district. Thus about 3/4 of the district can be regarded as the agricultural land or arable land. Rest of land of the district is non-arable accounting for about 30% of the land area.

Table 4.1
Vaishali District
Landuse (Figures in percent)

SI. No.	Types of landuse	1981	1991	2001
1.	Forest	-	-	-
2.	Barren and uncultivable waste land	9.05	6.27	12.62
3.	Land put to non-agricultural uses	13.02	16.90	16.21
4.	Cultivable waste land	0.09	0.23	0.18
5.	Permanent pastures and other grazing lands	0.13	0.14	0.20
6.	Miscellaneous tree crops grooves and orchards	2.85	3.51	4.90

7.	Other fallow lands excluding current fallow	1.00	0.76	0.28
8.	Current fallow	4.61	7.43	3.31
9.	Net sown area	69.22	64.84	62.30

Source : Directorate of Statistics and evaluation, Govts. of Bihar, Patna.

If we compare the ratio of Net sown area of district with the state of Bihar as well as with that of the country these are about 43% and 46% respectively. Hence we find that the area is purely agricultural. This is because of the favourable physical conditions for the cultivation of a number of crops. The favourable physical as well as climatic condition which has in turn into high degree of Intensity in Agriculture .The maximum ratio of land is being used for the cultivation of food crops to meet the ever rising demands for food. Therefore, the pressure on land for the cultivation of food crops has been increasing for the last several years. The extension of agricultural land has more or less reached the climax. All these situations suggest that a purely subsistence nature of Forming is being practiced in which excessive stress is on growing food crops.

If anchal wise situations are analysed it is observed that five anchals have more than 70% of their total area under N.S.A. There are Goraul (80.58%), Mahua (79.55%), Jandaha (73.03%), Lalganj (78.83%) and Patepur (70.35%). These high ratio of N.S.A. are found because these anchals are relatively fertile and there is safety from flood to a great extent. Other anchals have ratio raging between 60%-70%. These are Hajipur Vaishali, Sahdair Bujurg, Mahnar, Bidupur, Desri, Bhagwanpur, Chehrakalan, Patheri Belsor & Rajapakar. In these anchals lower rate of Net sown area could by attributed to either increasing urban influence or more flood water logging. The anchal of Raghopur is an exception where the ratio of N.S.A. is as low as 31.99%. This is because of the fact that the entire anchal is sandy in nature and the frequency of flood in very high. More than 3/4th of the total area comes under the grip of Ganga water every year during the rainy season. The sandys soil is not suitable for various crops and thus greater part remains and uncultivated.

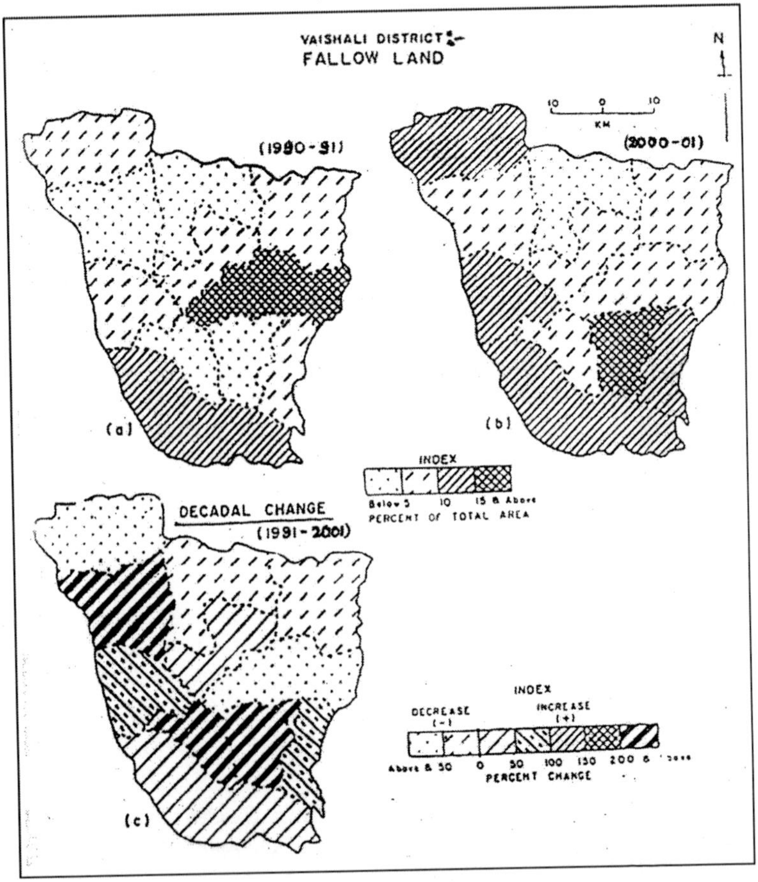
VAISHALI DISTRICT
FALLOW LAND
N
10 0 10
KM
(1990-91)
(2000-01)
(a)
(b)
INDEX
Below 5 10 15 & Above
PERCENT OF TOTAL AREA
DECADAL CHANGE
(1991-2001)
(c)
INDEX
DECREASE (-)
INCREASE (+)
Above & 50 0 50 100 150 200 & Above
PERCENT CHANGE

Fig. 4.1

So far as the spatial pattern of N.S.A. in Vaishali district in 2001 is concerned it is observed that the entire northern part except Vaishali anchal comprising the anchals of Lalganj, Goraul, Mahua, Patepur and Jandaha have a higher ratio of N.S.A. The ratio decreases towards south since the influence of flood. Thus floods are major hindrance in the N.S.A. of the Vaishali district.

Fallow lands are suitable for cultivation but not being used for cultivation continuously. It is so because cultivation makes the soil infertile. Thus, land is kept under fallowing for a certain period which is decided by the farmers. There are two types of fallow lands (i) current fallow and (ii) other follow.

These land are which have been kept fallow for one your while the other fallow lands are those in which cultivation has not been done for more than one year. Though, fallowing is done mainly for maintaining the fertility of the soil, there might be some other reasons too, which compel farmers to keep the land under fallowing.

The total area under fallowing in the Vaishali district is about 19,003,00 hectares during 2001 which comes to about 3.59% of the total land when compared to the state of Bihar and India respectively it is 16.06% and 8.08%. Thus the ratio of follow lands in the district is much less than that of Bihar and India's total average.

Non-Arable Land :

These are groups of land which can not be brought under cultivation without making radical changes. Cultivable waste land are virtually a wasteland due to a number of limitations viz. water-logging, weed jungle, Barrenland, sandy lands, land under tanks and marshes. Lands under non agricultural use are those which are occupied by building roads, railways, canals and settlements. Lands under forest cover, permanent pastures and grazing land, land under miscellaneous tree crops groves and orchards are grouped under non-arable land. These are discussed in following paragraphs separately.

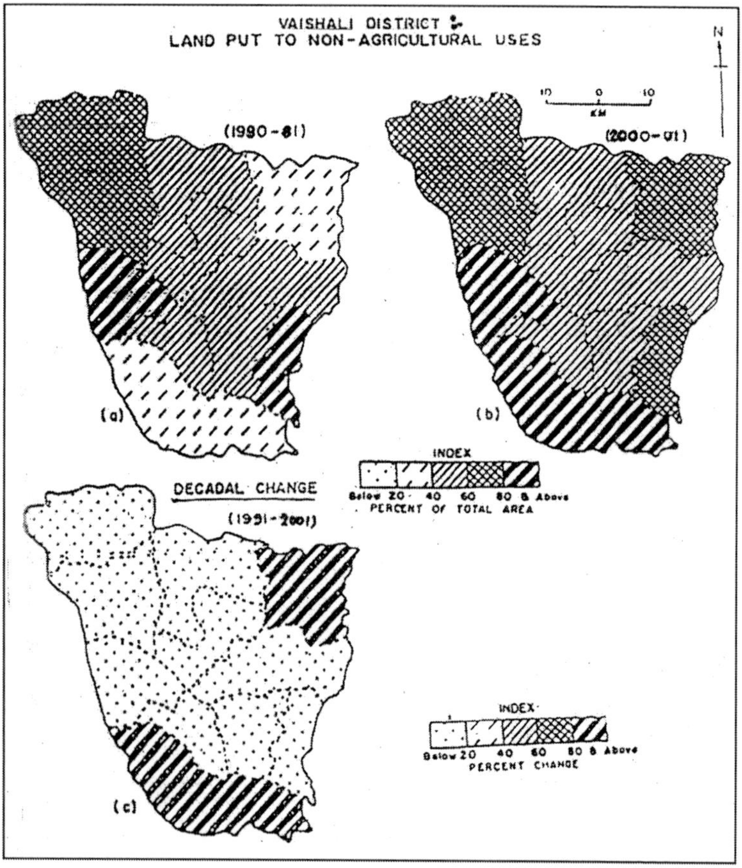
VAISHALI DISTRICT :-
LAND PUT TO NON-AGRICULTURAL USES
N
10 0 10
KM
(1980-81)
(2000-01)
(a)
(b)
INDEX
Below 20 40 60 80 & Above
PERCENT OF TOTAL AREA
DECADAL CHANGE
(1991-2001)
(c)
INDEX
Below 20 40 60 80 & Above
PERCENT CHANGE

Fig. 4.2

Land under Settlement and communication :

It is one of the most important utilization of land in this age of rapidly growing population. More and more lands are being required for the construction of houses, hospitals, roads, schools, roads, railways etc. Communication plays very important role in the development of any economy. It plays very important of collection and distribution of inland products. The agricultural products have to be moved to markets from far flung villages. Thus the movement of the commodities warrants a well efficient and co-ordinated means of transport & communication. For Vaishali being an agricultural district, if agriculture makes the body and bones of this district the communication is its nerves.

This district is served by a good network of transport and communication except, interior and diara areas. The North-Eastern railways serve the district and important stations are Hajipur, Muzaffarpur, Desri, Bidupur, Mahnar etc. The total length of railway tracks in the district is 71 kms. The district is also served by National and State Highways and other roads. The total length of roads in the district is about 3294 kms. Hajipur anchal is the most communicable anchal of the district which has connections from the whole of country through East-Central Railway and N.H. 19, N.K. 30, it is also well connected through river Ganga.

The land under settlement varies in the district's anchals. Mahnar (19.96%), Lalganj (18.88%) and Patepur (18.80%) are important anchals in respect of land under settlement. In the anchal of Vaishali, the ratio (16.41%) is about the same as for the district average. The maximum ratio of Hajipur (28.35%) is due to its proximity to the state capital Patna. It should be noted that a large part of Hajipur anchal is now under Patna regional development Authority (PRDA). The higher ratio of these land in Raghopur anchal has also been caused by the vicinity of Patna. Thus it is being observed that the proximity to any large or small town has contributed to the greater commercial value of land for the purpose of non-agricultural use. This is one of the main reason for the

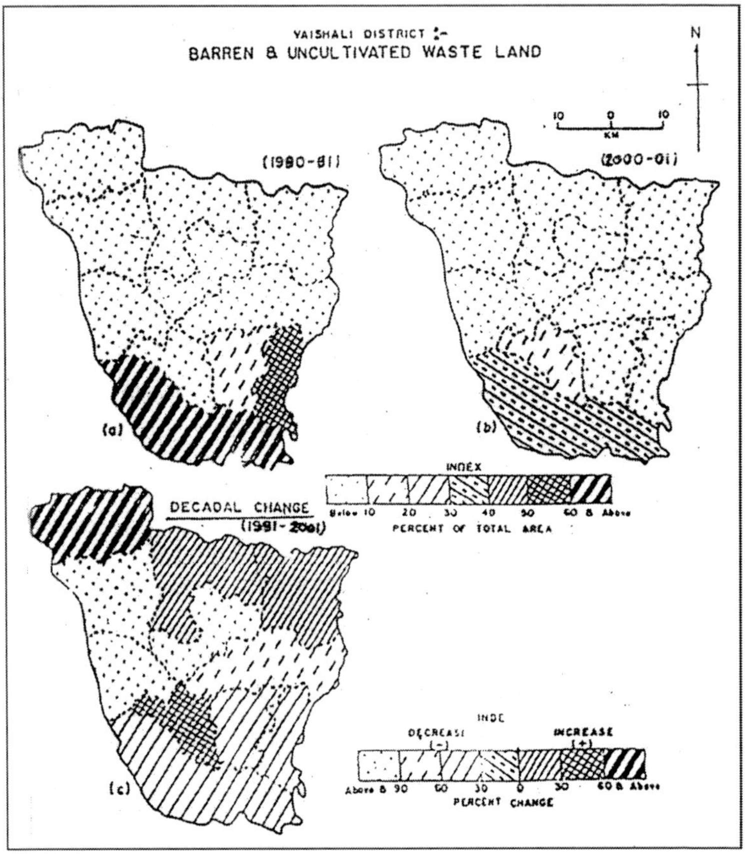
VAISHALI DISTRICT :-
BARREN & UNCULTIVATED WASTE LAND
N
10 0 10
KM
(1980-81)
(2000-01)
(a)
(b)
INDEX
Below 10 20 30 40 50 60 & Above
PERCENT OF TOTAL AREA
DECADAL CHANGE
(1981-2001)
(c)
INDE
DECREASE
(-)
INCREASE
(+)
Above & 90 60 30 0 30 60 & Above
PERCENT CHANGE

Fig. 4.3

higher ration of land put to non- agricultural use in the Vaishali district.

Barren and Uncultivated land :

It covers an area of about 59960 hectares accounting for 12.62% of the total area of the district. It is higher then the average ratio for Bihar (6.93%). These lands are mostly found in the vast sandy diara tracts. However, In other areas too, some lands remain barren and uncultivated for several reasons. The spatial pattern of this category of land in 2001 shows that the southern part of the district formed by the sandy diara tract of the Raghopur anchal has the maximum ratio (24.20%) while in some anchals there is no land under this category. These are Hajipur, Lalganj, Patepur, Mahua and Goraul.

This is because of greater ratio of land in these anchals are used for non-agricultural use. In Bidupur a sizeable amount (13.02%) of its area is under this category. It is because of its proximity to river Ganga which has deposited sands in its southern part making the land unfit for cultivation.

Land under Miscellaneous tree crops Groves and orchards :

The total area under this category of land is Vaishali district is about 23875 hectares which shares 4.90% of the total area of the district. This ratio is higher than the average for both Bihar and India in which it is 1.54% and 1.16% respectively. This is mainly because the plantation farming is on commercial scale is much higher than other regions of the state. The climate as well as the soil are very favourable for the cultivation of plantation crops especially Banana. The spatial patterns of this category of land however, is not uniform. Seven of the sixteen anchals have higher ratio of this land than the district average. These are Jandaha (5.92%), Patepur (5.28%), Vaishali (5.04%), Goraul (4.14%), Mahua (4.38%), Bhagwanpur (5.04%), Patheri Belsar (4.28%).

In the remaining anchals the pattern of this category of

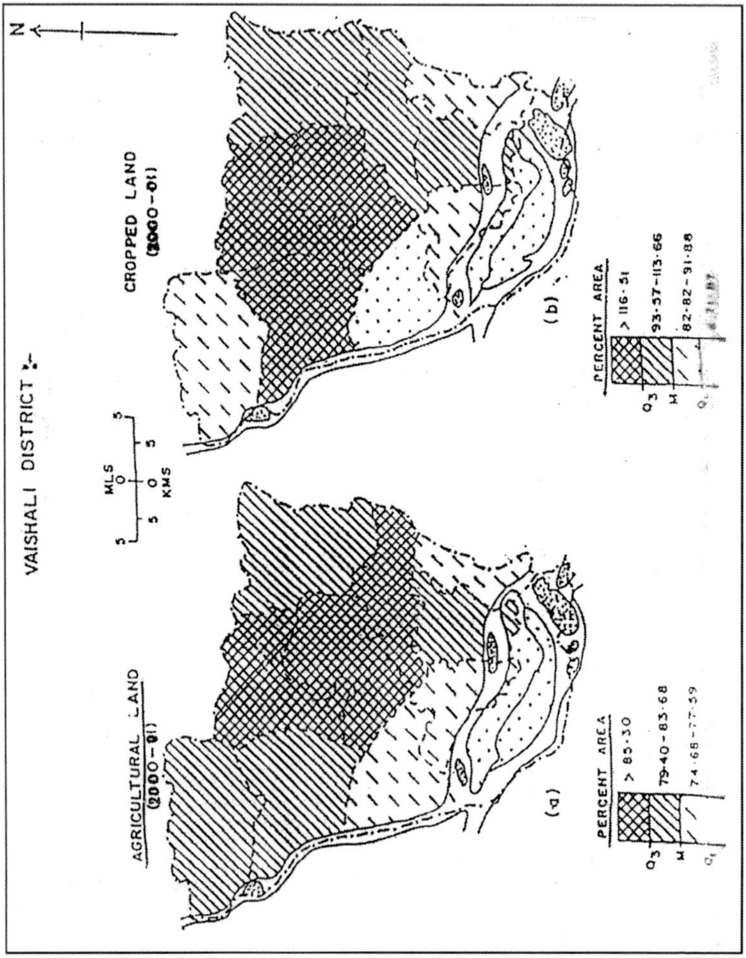
VAISHALI DISTRICT :-
N
MLS
KMS
AGRICULTURAL LAND (2000-01)
CROPPED LAND (2000-01)
(a)
(b)
PERCENT AREA
> 85·30
79·40 - 83·68
74·68 - 77·39
PERCENT AREA
> 116·51
93·57 - 113·66
82·82 - 91·88

Fig. 4.4

land is as follows – Lalganj (3.18%), Hajipur (2.62%), Sehdai Bujurg (1.93%), Bidupur (1.81%), Mahnar (1.58%), Raghopur (1.09%), Chehra kalan (2.03%), Desri (1.93%) and Raja Pakar (1.02%). Thus, we can see that the central part of the district has a higher proportion of land under this category, while in the southern and northern parts except North-western part, land ratio of this land is on a lower scale. This is mainly on account of the physiographic difference in different parts of the district.

Land Covered with Water or Cultivable Wasteland :

It covers the area of about 812 hectares accounting for only 0.18% of the total area of the district. These parts of the district face the problem of water logging. Thus these are not cultivated. However, these areas can be reclaimed for cultivation if suitable measures are taken to drain out the Stagnant water which remains in the field for a greater part of the year. The ratio of this land in Vaishali district is much lower than the state Bihar and India. Where it is 2.24% and 5.16% respectively. Thus, in Vaishali district this category of land is almost negligible. It appears in only three anchals of Raghopur (1.5%), Mahnar (0.34%) and Mahua (.06%). It clearly indicates that some measures for reclamation can be undertaken to cultivate in these wastelands.

Permanent pastures and other grazing land :

It covers very small area (898 hectares) of the district. The percentage share of this land in the district is only (0.20%). Pastures and other grazing lands were permanent features in the past when population was very thin. People during those days provided greater area to animals for grazing. But now-a-days the pressure of population on land is so high that pastures have become invisible.

So far as, the state of Bihar and the country are concerned the percentage of this land are 0.79% and 3.93% respectively. These figures also suggests that pastures and grazing land have become unimportant not only in Vaishali district but also in the state of Bihar and the country itself.

The spatial variation of this land also indicates its insignificant position. Of the total sixteen anchals nine do not have this category of land. Even the highest ratio (0.83%) in Raghopur is also less than 1%. In the remaining anchals this land is very rare. The insignificant position of pastures and other grazing land is an unhealthy sign for a developing economy. Greater attention should be given for providing adequate pastures to animals.

Pastoral farming is an important part of agriculture. In this age of rapid population growth, the development of pastoral farming can be of great help in solving the feed as well as nutrition problems, ultimately reducing the dependence on the grain crops. The above discussion on the various landuse types shows that forests are practically absent in this district. Its complete absence can be is quite obvious since it is densely populated district where forest have been cut for providing more land for agriculture to meet the demand for food since ancient times. However, in the state of Bihar and India forests account for 16.8% and 21.91% of their total areas respectively. This figures is even much below the required standard for the maintenance of proper ecological balance. Thus, it can be concluded that the pattern of landuse types in Vaishali district has been greatly influenced by the river rising population. In the present century with the passage of time, the rate of population growth has been increasing at an alarming rate. Thus it has formed the people to expand agricultural land. However, attempts have also been made to increase the food production. The N.S.A. (net sown area) has been increasing. At the same time, land put to non-agricultural uses has also recorded increased for the last several decades to meet its ever growing demand. This in turn poses a great difficulty in maintaining a balance between the rising population and the landuse types especially N.S.A and land put to non-agricultural uses.

Therefore decisions on changes in landuse should be made only after the present land is investigated from all viewpoints including cultural socio-economic and ecological conditions. Thus stamp has rightly observed "The land is the heritage rich natural beauty. Preservation is not inconsistent with effective utilization to make certain that we do not destroy out heritage but secure the best who will follow us.

Types of Land Capability :

The type and quality of the land is a major factor in the utilization of the land. In an agrarian economy the fertility of the soil is of utmost importance and it determines the cropping pattern on a large scale. The fertility of the soil is determined by the presence of chemical components like nitrogen, phosphorus, calcium etc. in different proportions. In fact, the fertility of the soil depends upon the presence of organic and inorganic substances. The role of organic substances however is more important. These substances are also called 'humus'. In the district of Vaishali three broad land capability types can be recognized. The classification of the land into various classes is based on a number of factors viz. location, accessibility, yield fertility, drainage, surface, gradient, Immunization from water logging etc.

Table 4.2
Vaishali District
Land Capability classes

Land Class	Class I land	Class II land	Class II land
1. Location	Around settlement	Near the settlement	For from settlement
2. Accessibility	Very good	Good	Poor
3. Yield (Index)	Very high	Moderate	Poor
4. Fertility	Very high	Moderate	Poor
5. Drainage	Very good	Moderate	Poor
6. Gradient	Higher site	Intermediate site	Lower site
7. Immunity from water logging	Always Immune	Sometimes water accumulates for brief Period	Water stagnates for longer time
8. Price Index	Rs. 1 lac/ hectare	Rs. 50,000-100000/- hectare	Below Rs. 50,000/- per hectare

Source : Directorate of Statistics and evaluation, Govts of Bihar, Patna.

Class I Lands :

These are found generally close to the settlement sites. However, a few exceptions can not be ruled out. Accessibility to these lands is generally very good and these are approached by pathways converging towards settlements. Being close to the settlement sites they remain always under the care and attention of the farmers. The soil are generally very fertile since these are being enriched by regular addition of human refuges and wastes. These wastes in addition, keep the land always higher than the surrounding areas. As a results drainage of these areas is always good and do not face the problem of water-logging. All of above features which are very favourable for cultivation as well as habitation, make these areas very costly and the price of these lands is generally above Rs. 1 lac for a hectare. These class I lands generally have multiple cropping in which mostly vegetables, grain crops like wheat, pulses and commercial crops like tobacco, spices etc are grown.

Class II Lands :

These lands are found near the settlement and in areas along some pathways, roads etc. The drainage is generally moderate and the soils have also moderate fertility. There are problems of water logging in some areas but water does not stay for longer period. These areas produce crops of all seasons. However, in the lower reaches of this area aghani crops are generally grown. The above characteristic feature of these lands have made their prices generally to range between Rs. 50,000-Rs. 1,00000 per hectare.

Class III Lands :

These lands are found generally away from the settlement sites. As a result, these do not remain under the care and attention of the farmers. These lands are relatively low hence, face the problems of water logging during rainy season water stagnant for a very long period of the year in these areas. This compels the farmers for not growing the aghani crops. However, some coarse crops of paddy are sown broadcast in some pockets of these lands. The fertility of the solid in areas which are visited by floods calcium. This is turn, makes the land very useful for the cultivation of Rabi crops.

However, in areas where there are accumulation of rain water, the fertility of soils is generally low. Hence, adequate amount of fertilizers are used for the cultivation of Rabi crops. The above characteristics features have made the price of lands generally below Rs. 50,000 for each hectare. The nature of spatial pattern of the land capability classes has been discussed in the light of Accesibility, communication, fertility, water logging and rural administration unit viz. Panchayat's parameters. Landuse may be used as an Index of socio-economic character of a region. Thus, it becomes an important device for the planner to use this index. Therefore, it is not only a vital tool but also an indispensable part of research.

References :

1. Singh, Jasbir and Dhillon, S.S. : Agriculture geography. Tata Mcgraw hill, limited, New Delhi, 1962, p. 326.
2. Best R.H. and Coppock, J.T. : The changing use of land in Britain (Reber and Reber) London 1962, p. 223.
3. Stamp L.D. (1960) : Applied Geography
4. Stamp L.D. : In the forward of "The Changing use of land in Britain". p. 14.
5. Goel G.S. and Ojha R.N. (1957) : Agricultural landuse in Punjab-A spatial analysis, New Delhi.
6. Singh Jasbir and Dhillon S.S. : Agricultural geography. Tata Mcgraw Hill Limited, New Delhi, 1982, p. 325.
7. Chang, Jen-her (1968) : 'The agriculture potential of the humid tropics', The geographical review. Vol. 58, No. 3.
8. Vink A.P.A. (1975) : Landuse in advancing and agriculture, Newyork, P. 1.
9. Stamp L.D. : In the forward of "The changing use of land in Britain, p. 16.
10. Hartshorne, R. (1939) : The nature of Geography (Association of American Geographers), p. 454.

11. Singh, J. (1975) : An agricultural Atlas of India : A Geographical Analysis, Vishal Pub, Kurukshetra, Haryana.

12. Shafi, M. (1960) : Land Utilization in Eastern UP, Aligarh, p. 48.

13. Mukherjee, R.K. (1939) : The changing face of Bengal, A study in rural economy, Calcutta, p. 239.

5

General Pattern of Landuse

Agricultural landuse is the most important form of resource utilization in Vaishali district. Being a part and parcel of the Gangetic plain, the district is predominantly an agricultural tract and will remain so for years to come. The nature of landuse has been changing owing to a change in the socio-cultural and economic situations. It is, therefore, obligatory to make an assessment of the vital aspects of agricultural landuse which a geographers can do by portraying the features on a map and presenting some relevant explanations. "The task of the agricultural geographer is the delimitation and assessment of the national characteristics of agriculture."

The work of an agriculture geographer, therefore, is more

Source: bhuwanchand.files.wordpress.com/2012/03/women-in-agriculture-india10.jpg

challenging and enterprising because it takes into all aspects including biological, social, cultural and economic conditions which exert their influence in the emergence of a characteristic pattern of agricultural landuse. It takes into account various aspects of economic geography viz. production, index, supply and demand, marketing, infrastructural growth, input status, agricultural land policy etc.

In the foregoing paragraphs an attempt has been made for a systematic study and careful interpretation of the various aspects of the agricultural landuse in Vaishali district. The four physical determinants of agriculture temperature, rainfall, topography and soil have already been analysed in the preceding chapter but other characteristics are still to be traced.

Arable Land :

It comprises of Net sown area, current follow land and land under other follows. It is about 70% of the total area of district. The Net sown area is about 63% of the district, as ever rising population requires food crops for food. The extension of land has more or less reached the climax. Anchalwise if situation is analysed it is observed that out of sixteen anchals five have a N.S.A. of more than 70%, Ten of them have N.S.A. of 60-70%. Only Raghopur anchal has less N.S.A. less than 40% of the total land area. The above facts suggest that arable land in the district is fully utilized and it has reached its extension.

Seasonal cropping :

Seasonal cropping is the main agricultural practice of the region. The agricultural year is divided into two main season, i.e., Kharif, the season of summer crops and rabi, the season of winter crops. Based on harvesting periods the agricultural year of the district is classed under the following heads :

Bhadai - Early Monsoon crops

Kharif or Aghani - Winter or end Monsoon crops

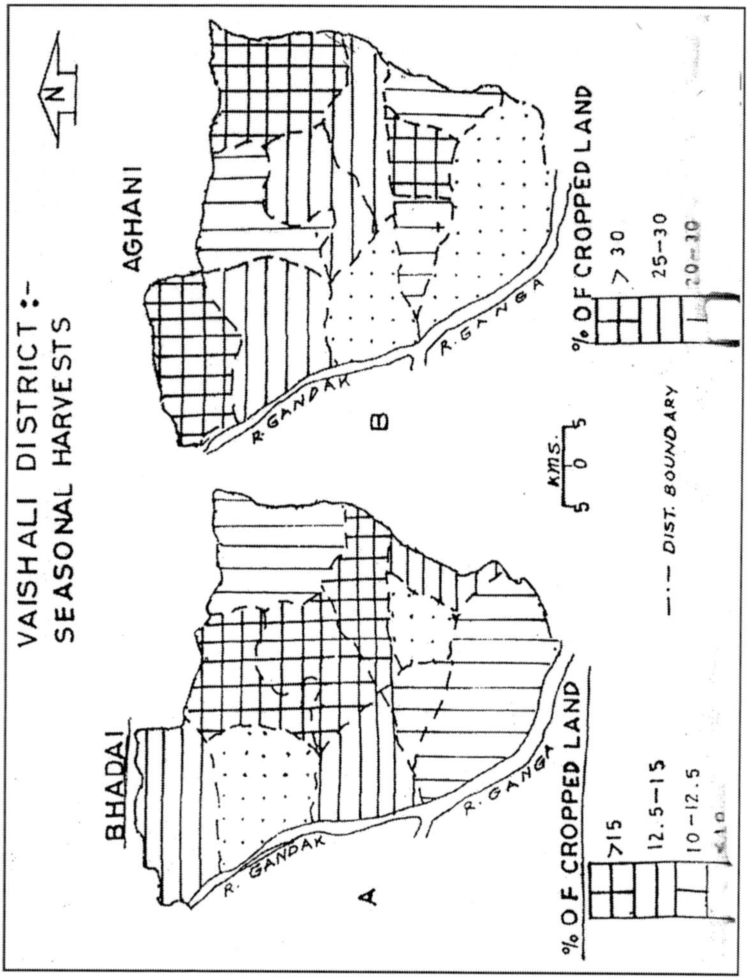
VAISHALI DISTRICT :-
SEASONAL HARVESTS
N
BHADAI
AGHANI
A
B
R. GANDAK
R. GANGA
KMS.
5 0 5
DIST. BOUNDARY
% OF CROPPED LAND
>15
12.5–15
10–12.5
% OF CROPPED LAND
> 30
25–30

Fig. 5.1

Rabi - Spring crops

Garma - Summer crops

1. Aghani or Kharif Crops :

These crops are sown in July-August and harvested in December-January. Aghani crops mainly includes Paddy, millets, Moong sugarcane etc. since these crops are harvested in winter season (Aghan) these are also known as winter crop. Paddy is the chief crop and its maximum production comes from this single season. Monsoon rains (July-August) are very important for transplantation of paddy. They are important not only in the sense that they contribute to the brighter prospects of Aghani crops but they also supplement the required moisture for the cultivation of Rabi crops.

2. Rabi Crop :

The next season of Rabi crops is important because wheat comes next to Rice as a food crop is grown chiefly in this season. Other crops of this season are pulse, oilseeds and spices etc. These are sown in October and harvested till end of March Rabi crops remains in the field during winter season which is almost dry, irrigation becomes inevitable. Besides that other infrastructural facilities including use of chemical fertilizers are also required. Recently introduced hybrid seeds are responsible for increased production of Rabi crops.

Although, Rabi crops do not require much water but two three light showers during the period prove very beneficial for the high yield of the crop.

3. Garma Crops :

These crops are sown in the later part of February and harvested in April-May. These crops have been recently introduced and becoming very popular. Since these crops are known as 'garma', the summer months are mostly dry and thus irrigation becomes essential, making the cultivation costlier. Though this season does not produces much quantity of crops but it is important for growing a number of crops like maize, mango, Bhindi, Kaddu, Parwals etc. others fruits like tarbuz, kharbuj and Kakri are grown mostly in the diara tracts where water table is high and soil moisture present.

4. Bhadai Crops :

The season begins in the months of May-June and continues till the end of August-September. The sowing of Bhadais crops depends entirely on the arrival of the monsoon rains. Thus a greater variation is noticed in the sowing and harvesting period of Bhadai crops. This season also grows a number of crops like Sathirice, Marua, Maize, urad, til, Jowar etc. Millet is also grown in the diara tracts where soil moisture is high. The soil moisture relieves the former of the dependence on the arrival of Monsoon rains and therefore, the millet in this region is sown much earlier i.e. in the month of April-May. The Sathi as the name suggests is ready for harvesting in just 60 days.

Table 5.1
Vaishali District
Seasonal Harvests

Season	Area under cultivation (hectare)		% of NSA		% of T.S.A	
	1990-91	2000-01	1990-91	2000-91	1990-91	2000-01
Aghani	53680	58311	41.08	42.37	27.97	28.22
Rabi	73550	76229	56.31	57.32	38.34	38.96
Garma	38218	40525	29.26	34.70	19.92	20.00
Bhadai	26409	23092	20.22	19.48	13.77	12.80
Total	191857	198157	146.87	153.87	100	100

Source : Directorate of Statistics and Evaluation, Govts of Bihar, Patna.

Distribution and Production of various crops :

In Vaishali district about 1.98 lakh hectares of land is cropped. Out of this 0.76 lakh hectare are under Rabi crops, 0.58 lakh hectares under kharif crops, 0.40 lakh hectares under

Garma crops and 0.23 lakh hectares under Bhadai crops. In this way, Rabis harvest is the most significant accounting for about 38% of the total cropped areas Aghani harvest ranks second with about 28% of the cropped area. Garma and Bhadai crops are less significant covering 20% and 13% of the cropped area respectively. In this way about 2/3rd of the cropped area is under Rabi and Aghani harvests and only 1/3 is under Garma and Bhadai harvests.

The area under different harvest varies from place to place. Table 5.2 shows the regional variation in distribution of different harvests in the district. In Bhadai crops, Goraul, Jandaha, Mahua, Desri covering north central and east central part of the district are rich. These areas are very fertile where Bhadai crops are grown without irrigation. On the other hand the flood prone areas of Raghopur, Bidupur, Patepur, Sahdai Bujurg and Lalganj are poor in Bhadai crops.

Aghani crops rank second after Rabi in the district. The flood free areas having irrigation facilities are rich in aghanis harvests while the flood prone areas are poor.

Rabi is the most significant harvest of Vaishali district covering about 76 thousand hectares or 38% of the cropped area of the district. Flood prone areas of Sahdai Bujurg, Hajipur, Raja Pakar are significant in Rabi crop. In these anchals 40%-46% of the cropped land is under Rabi harvest on the other hand, Goraul, Lalganj and Bidupur are poor in Rabi poor.

Garma crops occupies about 40 thousands hectares of land which is about 20% of the total cropped areas of the district. In this crop areas which have better irrigation facilities are very significant. Birupur, Mahnar, Hajipur are important garma crop area while Sahdai Bujurg and Vaishali are very poor.

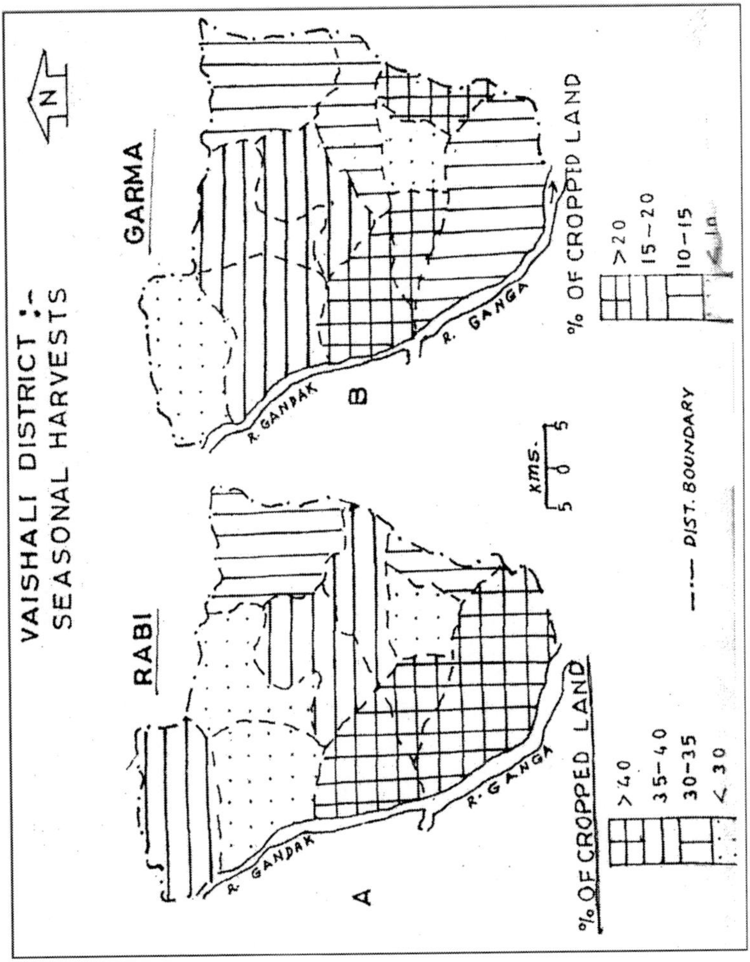
VAISHALI DISTRICT :-
SEASONAL HARVESTS
N
RABI
GARMA
A
B
R. GANDAK
R. GANGA
R. GANDAK
R. GANGA
KMS.
5 0 5
DIST. BOUNDARY
% OF CROPPED LAND
>40
35-40
30-35
< 30
% OF CROPPID LAND
>20
15-20
10-15

Fig. 5.2

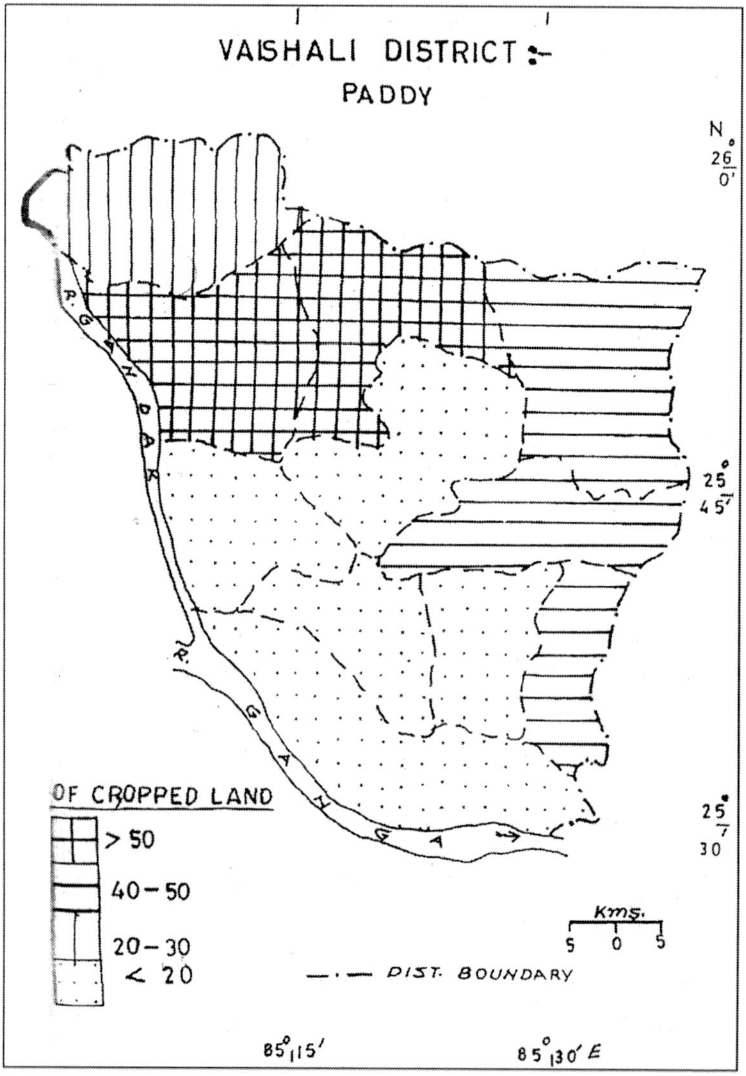
VAISHALI DISTRICT :-
PADDY
N
26°
0'
25°
45'
25°
7
30
R. GANDAK
R. GANGA
OF CROPPED LAND
> 50
40 – 50
20 – 30
< 20
Kms.
5 0 5
DIST. BOUNDARY
85° 15'
85° 30' E

Fig. 5.3

Table 5.2
Vaishali District
Regional Variations in various crops 2000-01

SI. No.	Name of the Anchals	Bhadai	Aghani	Rabi	Garma
1.	Hajipur	1348.65	2812.36	5348.53	2470.56
2.	Bidupur	1295.49	2830.11	4928.08	2308.18
3.	Vaishali	1830.24	6852.08	4803.29	1788.86
4.	Lalganj	1848.22	7651.36	6832.92	5177.48
5.	Goraul	3022.31	6536.21	9381.46	4254.98
6.	Mahua	3177.18	5640.22	9632.42	3861.31
7.	Patepur	1865.46	7321.84	5388.73	4500.86
8.	Jandaha	855.32	3458.31	5837.58	4008.31
9.	Mahnar	1221.35	2835.27	3912.61	3119.02
10.	Sehdai Bujurg	1027.00	3847.18	6322.67	2498.92
11.	Raghopur	808.28	823.02	3211.56	1609.51
12.	Raja pakar	893.28	1228.39	2255.92	1217.04
13.	Desri	1101.32	2243.58	2453.88	897.62
14.	Chehra kalan	823.28	1632.18	2141.78	1287.92
15.	Patheri Belsar	1226.03	1334.68	2824.76	699.01
16.	Bhagwanpur	748.12	1255.21	1951.91	825.00
	Total	**23092**	**58311**	**76229**	**40525**

Source : Self computation based on various sources of data.

Principal Crops :

The most important crops of the district are paddy, wheat, barley, maize, vegetables, gram, sugarcane, potato, banana etc. other crops of the region are khesari, arhar, chillies, andi, oilseeds, pulses etc. These crops are cultivated in different harvesting seasons.

Paddy : Winter Paddy

Winter paddy is the most important aghani crop. This crops depends heavily on monsoon rains. It is grown in poor quality land while the finest variety of paddy is cultivated on good quality land and coarse rice is grown in chaur land. Medium quality land produces medium quality rice. In 1990-91 the area under paddy measured over 60,000 hectares while in 2001 it was 49,000 hectares which is 90% of the cropped

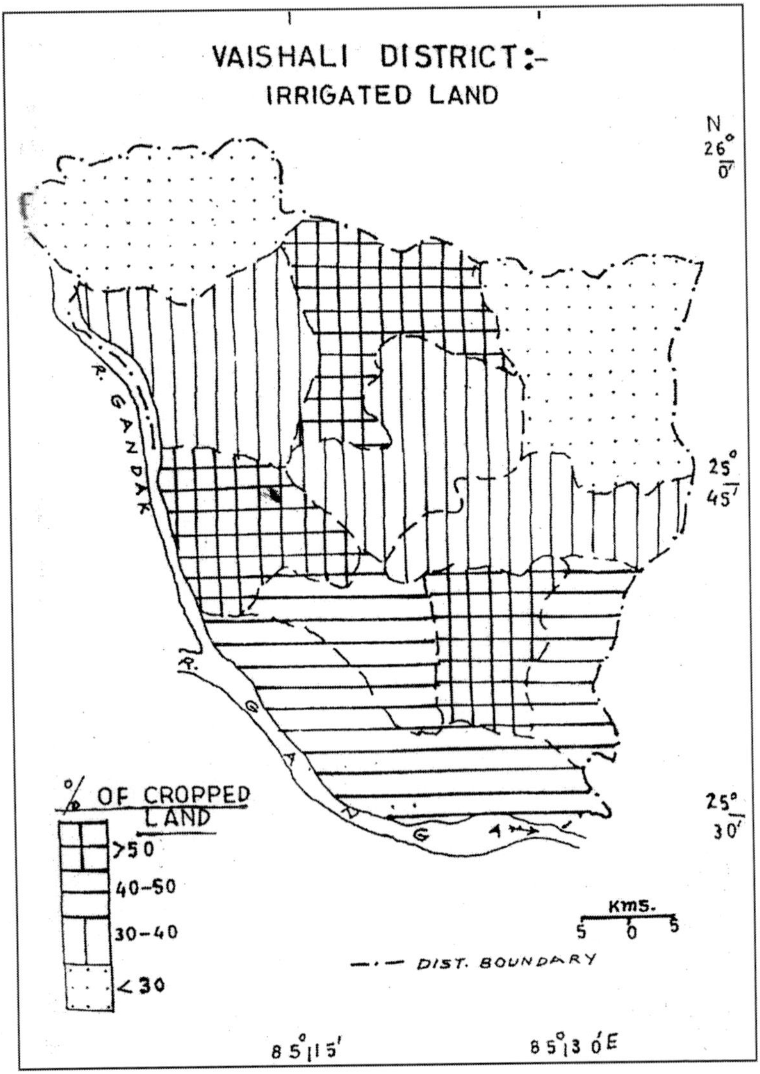
VAISHALI DISTRICT:-
IRRIGATED LAND
N
26°
0'
25°
45'
25°
30'
R. GANDAK
R. GANDAK
% OF CROPPED LAND
>50
40-50
30-40
<30
Kms.
5 0 5
DIST. BOUNDARY
85°15'
85°30'E

Fig. 5.4

area under aghani harvest. However, paddy harvesting is not reliable and a higher degree of fluctuation is involved. It is because of the irregularly of monsoon rains in the regions. Paddy cultivation is again considered to be a relatively easier task right from growing the seedlings to the final threshing and milling. Agricultural workers feel psychologically half hungry if their diet does not include rice. Therefore paddy cultivation is taken very seriously, mobilizing all possible resources at the disposal of the farmers. It is believed that the cultivation of rice has been the main reason for rapid growths of population.

Paddy is cultivated by two methods transplantation method and broadcast method. Broadcast method of paddy is grown in mainly chaur lands. Paddy seeds are sown in the dry chaur land in the months of April and May. In the heavy clayey soils paddy plants germinates quickly with the first shower of the pre-monsoonal rains. The low lying chaur land are flooded in quite early monsoon showers but the fast growing paddy plants keep pace with a rising level of water, sometimes plants are drowned for a few days, they withstand temporary drowning. The plants grows like creepers, baroban, Zemra, dasaria etc. are some of the important varieties of paddy grown in low land.

Transplantations paddy is grown in good quality land, Dhanhar and bhits land, while broadcast paddy does not requires constant irrigations, it is irrigated at least once. In dry monsoon's years usually upland rice of bhith withers away complete because of the farmers can not afford to irrigate due to higher cost of irigation. The basmati, Sitwa, kalamdam, mansuria, shyamzira, zakajira etc are very good quality of rice. It is grown in fertile Dhanhar and Bhit lands. As most of the medium quality paddy (taichung, I.R.8 etc.) all high yielding varieties and others are grown in medium qualities land (Dhanhar lands). Yield of paddy very from 800kg – 1000kg per hectares in the region. While the grains constitutes the staple food, the paddy stalks provide important food for domestic animals and serve also as building materials in rural areas. In true sense aghani paddy forms the basis of the entire rural economy of Vaishali district. Moreover, during the months of October-November when water in the Dhanhar lands starts drying up a variety of mud fish is caught in abundance. Thus, rice and fish grown together particularly in low lying fields, furnish ideal non-vegetarian diet to the people of the region.

Among the three harvests of paddy Aghani paddy is the most significant followed by bhadai and garma paddy. In the production of paddy Northern part of the district is significant. In Lalganj, Vaishali, Patepur, Patheri Belsar, Mahua Goraul anchals paddy cultivations is above 90% of the NSA during Aghani crop. The lowest ratio of paddy cultivation is found in Raghopur anchal (76.41%). It is because of the sandy soil and infrastructural deficiency. Garma paddy is grown in Jandaha, Mahnar, Desri, Sahdai Bujurg and Lalganj anchals.

Wheat :

Wheat is an important staple food of this region and stands second in production and cultivation hectarage. It is usually sown at the end of October and ripens in March and April. It is mostly cultivated in bhit (good quality lands) wheat is generally cultivated on Bhadai fields which remain follow during the kharif season. Seasonal following is supposed to enable the field to region soil fertility. In the year 2001 wheat covered total area of 48024 hectares and accounted for 25% of the total cropped land of the region. The yield range from 400-800 kg per hectare depending upon the inputs mainly hybrid seeds, Manures, fertilizers and irrigation facilities. The spatial pattern of wheat cultivation shows that out of the total sixteen anchals seven northern anchals have higher ratio of land under wheat cultivation. These are Bidupurs (84.81%), Lalganj (79.32%), Patepur (65.97%), Hajipur (79.29%), Patheri Belsar (80.31%) Vaishali (62.01%), Raghopur (78%) other anchals have lower ratio of land under wheat.

Maize :

Maize is one of the staple food of people of the region. It is one of the leading Bhadai crop of the district Vaishali. The total area under maize in 2001, was 24212.58 hectares which accounted for 12.85% of the total cropped area. Maize is sown in the first shower of Monsoon in early. June and harvested in September. A long break in the rainfall or excessive fall and flood damage the crop. On the other hand, water-logging is also harmful, thus maize is not sown in the low lying areas. Lands which are high, well drained and loamy soiled are suited for the cultivation of maize. It is consumed by local people in enormous quantity. The green grains (bhutta) as well as the fried grains are consumed with great taste. It is regularly grown in diara area on the flood coming late to allow the crops being reaped. Maize is grown under Bhadai, Garma and Rabi seasons. Bhadai maize is the most important followed by Garma and Rabi maize. Bhadai maize is very significant in Mahua anchal with 20% of the total bhadai maize area of the district is located. In Rabi Maize Patepur leads with 28% of total Rabi maize area of the district. Other significant Rabi maize producer anchals are Raghopur (10.21%) and Goraul (8.80%). Garma maize requires 2-3 times irrigation in dry season thus it is cultivated in well irrigated anchals of Goraul, Mahua and Patepur.

Mung :

Mung is another important Garma crop grown in the district. It covers about 18000 hectares of land which is 9.5% of the cropped area of the district. Mung is an important pulse having high protein value. It is shown as a mixed crop with Bhadai maize. It requires no irrigation and can be raisedon less fertile land. This crop is also useful for green fodder as its leaves are used as fodder. About 21,109 metric tones of mung was grown in 2001 in the district. The Goraul anchal has 21% of the mung producing area of the district. Mahua, Patepur, Jandaha are other Mung growing areas.

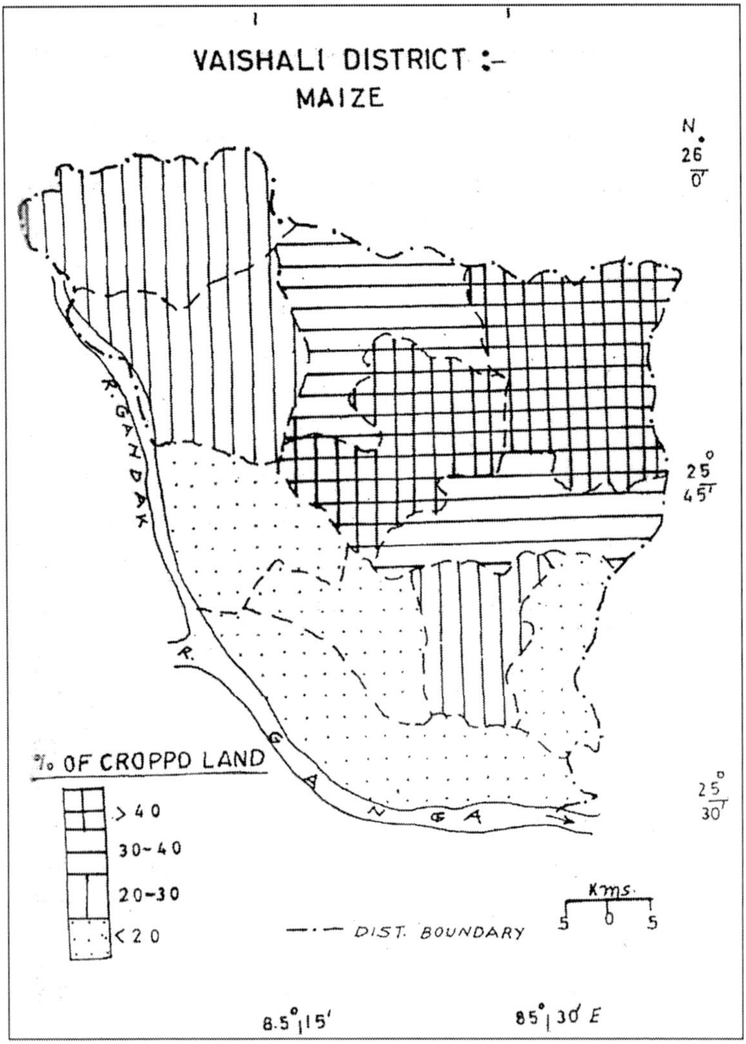
VAISHALI DISTRICT :-
MAIZE
N
26°
0'
25°
45'
25°
30'
R. GANDAK
R. GANGA
% OF CROPPD LAND
> 40
30-40
20-30
< 20
DIST. BOUNDARY
Kms.
5 0 5
85° 15'
85° 30' E

Fig. 5.5

Tobacco :

It is most important commercial crop of Rabi season in this district. It covers an area of 7607 hectares accounting for 9.34% of the total area under Rabi crops in 2001. Tobacco farming is increasing in the district as it is immediately sold after harvesting and they get good income. Anchals which are important for tobacco cultivation are Jandaha (26.32%), Goraul (28.84%) and Mahua (20.52%).

Oilseeds :

The include mainly linseed and mustard. However, other oilseeds such as castor, kusum etc. are also cultivated in some parts of the district. The total area under oilseed cultivation in year 2001 was 1979 hectares accounting for 2.46% of the total area under Rabi crops. Highest ratio of oilseed production is found in the anchal of Mahua (4.6%) while the lowest ratio is found in Mahnar (1.36%).

Vegetables :

Vegetables cover 10500 hectares of land of the district. It accounts for 6.73% of the total cropped area. A large number of vegetables are grown in the district. These are grown during all the four harvests seasons. But Rabi vegetables and Aghani vegetables are more important occupying 2.32% and 1.58% of the cropped area of the district respectively. Garma vegetables accounts for about 1.32% of the cropped area followed by Bhadai vegetable (0.98%), Rabi vegetables consists of potato, brinjal, tomato and cauliflower. Garma vegetables are parwal, bhindi, torai, brinjal, karailla and parwals. The maximum ratio of land under green vegetable during Rabi seasons is found in Mahnar anchals. Other important anchals for vegetable production are Desri and Raghopur.

Pulse :

A Large varieties of pulses are cultivated in the district. These are gram, arhar, masoor, khesari and urad. These pulses are grown under all the four harvesting seasons, but

Rabi pulse is the most significant occupying about 3200 hectares of land. Garma pulse includes Mung and Urad. In the areas under Rabi pulse Mahua, Lalganj and Vaishali are very important, but Hajipur and Bidupur and poor. In Bhadai pulse Jandaha, Mahua Vaishali are significant in Urad and gram and Raghopur and Hajipur in Mung.

Banana :

Banana is a nutritious and popular fruit. In comparison to other fruits, it provides more balanced diet. Its plantation is very easy. In Bihar Banana cultivation is done in all the districts but Vaishali comes first in terms of area under plantations and production. It is mainly cultivated in the southern anchals of Hajipur Bidupur, Raghopur, Desri and Mahnar. It requires loamy soil or sandy-loamy soil for plantation.

The proper irrigation of the plantation and drainage is beneficial for growths of banana plantations. The banana of Hajipur is very popular all over India. The important varieties of banana grown in the region are 'Batisa', 'bankel', kachkel' 'singhal', 'viula', 'bhons' etc. These are mainly used as vegetables. 'Alpan', 'malbhog', 'chinia', 'champa', 'kanthali', 'Rajabajai', Barsai, harichhal and kasturi etc. are important varieties of banana for fruit.

Sugarcane :

It is an early crop and harvested in the months of December-January. But it has been included in the Bhadai crop of the district by the Directorate of Statistics and evaluation, Vaishali and thus it has been analysed as Bhadai crop. The cultivation of sugarcane is for purely commercial purpose. It supplies raw material for sugar factories situated in and around the district boundaries. Small amount are also used in making 'gur' and 'khandsari' in rural areas. Unfortunately for the last several years sugarcane cultivation is on the decline, due to various reasons. Sugarcane is produced by small farmers and they need immediate money but mill owners take time. Mills are also closing rapidly due

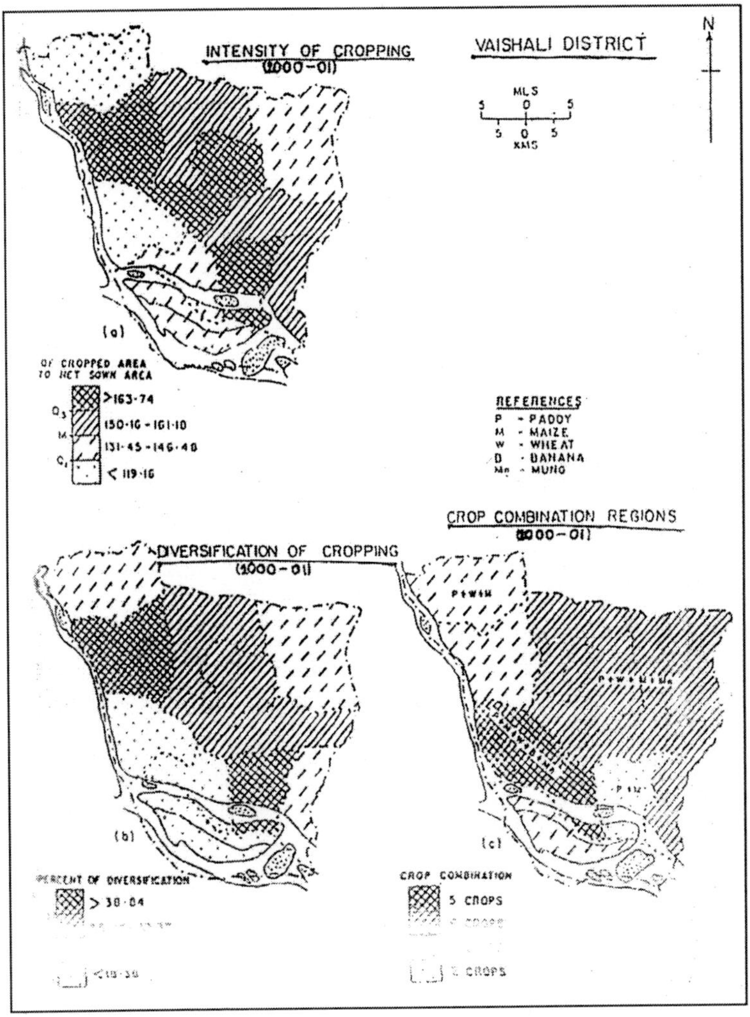
INTENSITY OF CROPPING
(2000-01)
VAISHALI DISTRICT
N
MLS
5 0 5
5 0 5
KMS
(a)
OF CROPPED AREA TO NET SOWN AREA
>163·74
150·16 - 161·10
131·45 - 146·48
< 119·16
REFERENCES
P - PADDY
M - MAIZE
W - WHEAT
B - BANANA
Mn - MUNG
CROP COMBINATION REGIONS
(2000-01)
DIVERSIFICATION OF CROPPING
(2000-01)
(b)
(c)
PERCENT OF DIVERSIFICATION
> 38·04
CROP COMBINATION
5 CROPS
CROPS

Fig. 5.6

to shortage of electricity and infrastructural facilities. Lalganj is the most important sugarcane producing anchal with (12.04%) of its area under Bhadai crops used to sugarcane cultivation. Other important anchals are Hajipur, Vaishali, Sahdai Bujurg, Mahnar etc.

Intensity of Agriculture :

The intensity of cropping implies the degree of cropping or the number of crops grown in the same plot during one agricultural year. It is on indication of the total cropped area as distinguished from the net sown area. This data becomes very useful as it shows the intensity of cropping. Such data also throws light on the possibilities or otherwise intensification of agriculture. The index of the intensity of cropping is calculated with the helps of following formula :

$$\text{Intensity of cropping} = \frac{\text{Total sown area (T.S.A.)}}{\text{Net sown area (N.S.A.)}} \times 100$$

Intensity of cropping depends upon environmental factors including relief, soil, climate, population etc. However, the infrastructural facilities and level of technical know how also influence the intensity of cropping to a great extent. In Vaishali district the environmental factors are basically responsible for the existing intensity of cropping. The fertile level land with favourable monsoon climate and a high degree of density of population have resulting into a high intensity of cropping.

In Vaishali district almost all anchals have very high index of Intensity of cropping. The highest figure is recorded in Sahdai Bujurg (172%) followed by Mahua and Lalganj (164%) each. On the other hand Vaishali (119%) and Hajipur (113%) have lowest intensity of cropping.

Crop Combination :

In a region where main occupation of the people is farming and where a variety of crop are grown owing to favourable geographical factors, the most suitable method

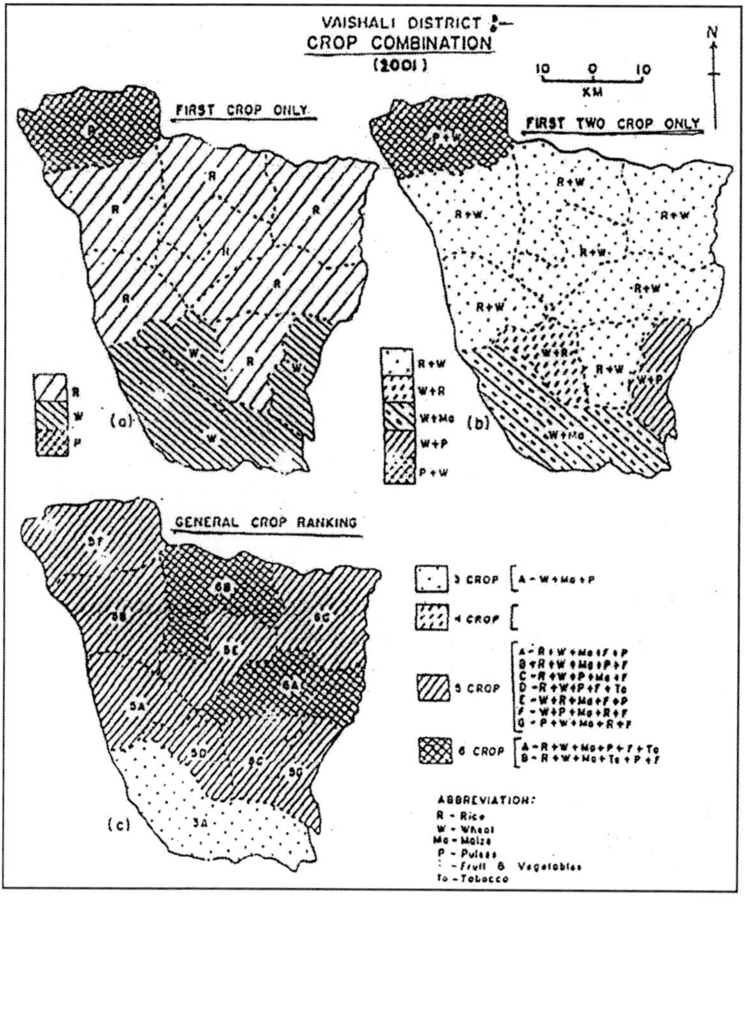
VAISHALI DISTRICT
CROP COMBINATION
(2001)
10 0 10
KM
N
FIRST CROP ONLY
FIRST TWO CROP ONLY
GENERAL CROP RANKING
(a)
(b)
(c)
R+W
W+R
W+Mo
W+P
P+W
3 CROP
4 CROP
5 CROP
6 CROP
ABBREVIATION:
R - Rice
W - Wheat
Mo - Maize
P - Pulses
To - Tobacco

Fig. 5.7

to divide the whole region into Micro regions to delineate the crop combination regions. It is one of the techniques of agricultural regionalization and forms a fundamental part in the study of geography which is mainly related to spatio-temporal analysis of phenomena. Agricultural regionalization is essential because it is intimately connected with the eradication of agricultural backwardness by rational allocation of new enterprises.

A region is always transitional in character since it can not be demarcated by a sharp boundary. However, a political boundary may be demarcated by boundaries which may serve also as the administrative boundaries. An agricultural region is entirely different from the surrounding and adjacent regions on the basis of physical, cultural and other characteristics. However, an agricultural region changes into another regions. Thus it becomes very difficult task for agricultural geographer to delimit the boundaries of an agricultural region. As Buchanan states "An extensives area of land with broadly similar conditions and pattern of agricultural practices distinctive from those of adjacent areas."

In the Vaishali district the physical as well as the climatic factors are most suitable for the cultivation of a variety of crops. The land has been used extensively and intensively for the cultivation of various crops. In these circumstance, for a proper any systemetic study of its dynamic agricultural pattern crop combination regions or cropping mosaic may be very useful.

Uptil now several techniques have been evolved to delineate the crop combination regions. Some of these techniques are "Minimum deviation method" (weaver). "Maximum deviation method" (Rafiullah), 'Doi's Method' etc. Although, the most commonly used technique known as arbitrary choice method also gives a very good picture of the agricultural regions based on area under different crops. In the present study agricultural regions are based on area under different crops. In the present study agricultural regions are based on first crop i.e. the crop having the highest area in any anchal. First two crops i.e. the two crops having the highest area under cultivation have been carved out.

Single cropping :

In Vaishali district lands under single cropping are being converted into multiple cropping to meet the growing demand of foodgrains but still a large part of the net sown area in this district is left under single cropping. In 2001 it measured total area of 58666 hectare sharing 48.29% of the N.S.A. Thus more than half of the N.S.A. is still left under this category of land and there is enough scope for increasing productions of foodgrains.

The spatial pattern of single cropping in Vaishali district shows that its ratio ranged between 41% in Jandaha anchal to 82% in Goraul anchals on analyzing the cropping pattern of last 20 years it is obvious that single cropping is becoming unpopular with farmers. They are putting greater attention towards multiple cropping to raise the production of foodgrains. These positive changes suggest that the state of agricultural development in the region is still in initial stage which has a large potential for greater intensities of cropping to get the maximum return from the land.

Paddy is the most important crop of Vaishali district occupying the maximum area wheat comes next. Paddy ranks first in Nine anchals of Vaishali district while wheat ranks first in five anchals and pulses ranks first in two anchals. In the southern part of the district Rabi crop is mostly dominating as during Aghani (Monsoon season) most of the areas are waterlogged and flooded. Aghani crop mainly paddy dominated in Northern part of the district where Monsoonal rain do not flood the fields due to highers position, rather it helps in the paddy cultivation. Anchals leading in Aghani crop are Hajipur, Lalganj, Mahua, Sahdai Bujurg, Patepur, Goraul, Raja Pakar, Chehra Kalan. Anchals leading in Rabi crop are Bidurpur, Desri, Mahnar, Raghopur, Jandaha etc.

Double Cropping :

Paddy and wheat dominate the whole Vaishali district. In Nine anchals the combinations of Paddy wheat rank the first position. A reverse combination of wheat+paddy is found in the anchals of Bidupur Desri and Sahdai Bujurg. Besides these to crops pulses and maize also find their place in the combination of two crops. The dominance of these two food crops reflects the subsistence nature of forming.

Triple Cropping :

In this cropping pattern three crops paddy + wheat + pulses dominates. In six anchals paddy + wheat + pulses combination has the positions of main crops. These anchals are namely Vaishali, Bidupur, Desri, Raja Pakar, Bhagwanpur and Lalganj.

Crop Combination Regions :

Vaishali is mainly an agriculturals economy where most of the people are involved in agriculture and here a variety of crops are grown. The most suitable method to divide the whole region into smaller regions is to delineate the crop combination regions.

It is one of the techniques of agricultural regionalization. Agricultural regionalization is very essential in order to eradicate backwardness of the region through rationale planning and its implementation. The works of scholars like whitlesey (1936), Halbum (1957), Kawachi (1959), Kostrovicky (1964) and Grigg (1965) have equipped the agricultural geographers with criteria or bases for quantitative classification of the diverse agricultural landscape.

A region is always transitional in characters and its is very difficult to demarcate a region by a sharp boundary. A geographical region which includes also the agricultural region can not change easily but the administrative regions could change with the change in political conditions. However an agricultural region changes gradually into another region. As Buchanan puts into his words – "Establishing the pattern of the agricultural region involves findings the best possible boundaries to the individual region, which in turn implied both definition and delimitation. The actual fixing of boundaries implies that the criterion must be capable of being plotted on a map." Thus we can define an agricultural region as the extensive area of land with broadly similar conditions and pattern of agricultural practices distinctive form those of adjacent areas."

In Vaishali district the physical as well as climatic factors are suitable for the cultivation of various crops. For a systematic study of its dynamic agricultural pattern of crop combination region or cropping mosaic may be very useful. For the study of the Vaishali district the most common technique of regionalization known as "arbitrary choice method" has been applied. In this method agricultural regions based on first crop i.e. the crop having the highest area in different anchals, first tow crops i.e. the two crops having the highest area under cultivation have been carved out.

During a span of ten years 1991-2001 some variation in the distribution of crops in different anchals have been observed. So far as only the first crop is concerned there is little variation. Paddy is the most important crop in the Vaishali district occupying the maximum area (49,000 hect) wheat comes next (48024 hect.). Paddy ranks first in Nine anchals, Hajipur, Mahua, Desri, Goraul, Raja pakar, Lalganj, Chehra kalan, Sahdai bujurg and Mahnar. In the combination of two crops paddy+wheat almost six anchals rank high. Crop combination have further been divided on the basis of three crop combination to six crops combination region. The detailed figure has been given in table 5.3.

Table 5.3
Vaishali District
Crop Combination regions

No.of Crops	Crop combination	No. of Anchals	Anhal's name
One crops	Paddy	1	Sahdai Bujurg
Two crops	Paddy+Wheat	1	Jandaha
Three crops	Paddy+Wheat+Pulses	2	Mahua, Goraul
Four crops	Wheat+Paddy+Maize+ Fruits & Vegetables	4	Patheri Belsar, Raja pakar, Ragopur, Desri
Five crops	Paddy+Wheat+Maize+ Fruits & Vegetable +Pulses	5	Lalganj, Bidupur, Vaishali, Hajipur
Six crops	Paddy+Wheat+Pulses+ Maize+Tobacco+Fruits & Vegetables	3	Mahnar, Bhagwan-pur, Patepur, Chehra kalan

Source : Based on figures available from the directorate of statistics and evaluation. Govt. of Bihar, Patna.

The changes in general crop ranking during the period 1981-1991 reflect a greater degree of diversification of agricultural crops. In 1991-2001 the combination of two crops and four crops which were in existence in 1981-1991 lost there place. The combination of five crops witnessed maximum increase since it has extended its area from six anchals to eight anchals in 1991-2001.

Now farmers are also paying their attention towards cultivation of commercial crops like sugarcane, Banana, Fruits and vegetables, pulses and tobacco in order to increase their income. It is a positive change in the agricultural scenario of the district.

Agricultural efficiency :

Vaishali has primarily an agricultural based economy, where more than 80% people have been involved in agriculture. Its soil is very fertile and there are plenty of water

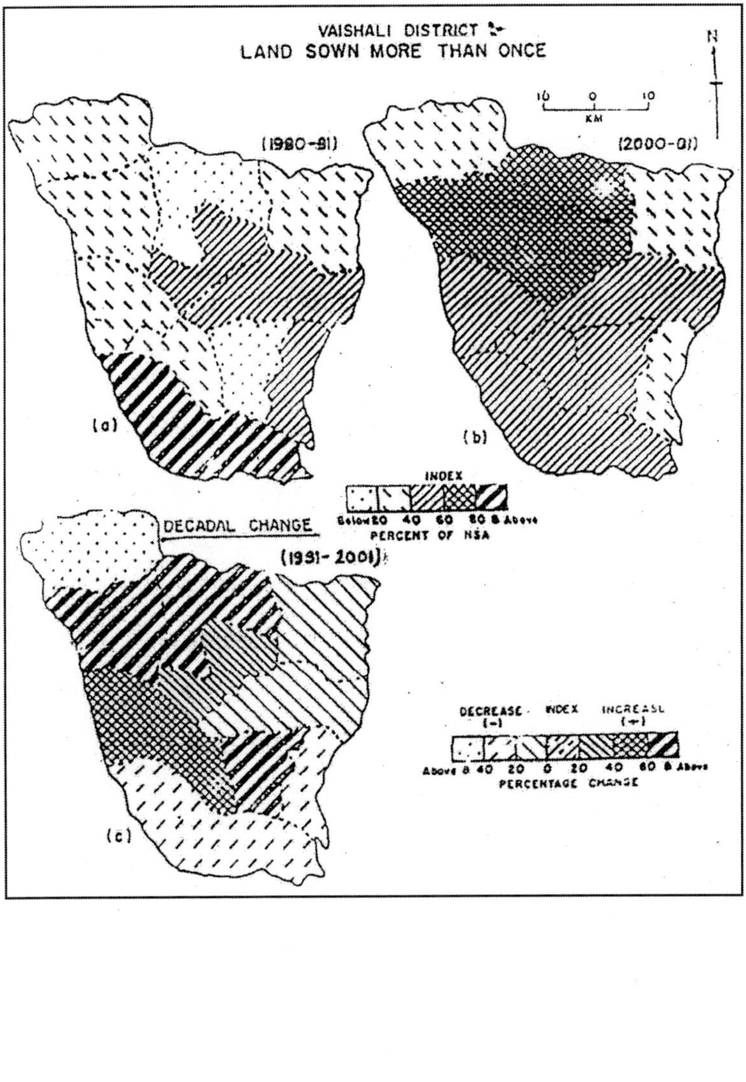
VAISHALI DISTRICT
LAND SOWN MORE THAN ONCE
N
10 0 10
KM
(1980-81)
(2000-01)
(a)
(b)
INDEX
Below 20 40 60 80 & Above
PERCENT OF NSA
DECADAL CHANGE
(1991- 2001)
DECREASE INDEX INCREASE
(-) (+)
Above & 40 20 0 20 40 60 & Above
PERCENTAGE CHANGE
(c)

Fig. 5.8

sources. Still the region ranks very low in terms of Agricultural efficiency. Agricultural efficiency of an area depends upon various factors involved in agricultural practices of that area, i.e. use of agricultural tools and machinery, irrigation facilities intensiveness of farming. The size of holdings, pressure of man on land, production of crops per hectare and subsistence or commercial character of agriculture. In Vaishali district a large number of farmers are still using old traditional farming equipments. Wooden plough and oxes used for tilling. The farmers gradually have become conscious of production and started to use modern implements which include mainly tractors, power tillers, threshers, Sprayers, dusters etc. Irrigation through tubewells and diesel pump sets are becoming popular. With the introduction of these modern implements the production of foodgrains has increased to some extent. At the same time it has also brought about same changes in the cropping pattern in some parts of the district.

Again the agricultural scenario of the district displays dismal picture. In respect of tractors and power tillers the number comes to only 0.20 for each hundred hectare of N.S.A other implements like sprayers and dusters are also used in some areas specially by well to do farmers. In Vaishali district as a whole the number of diesel pump sets for every one hundred hectare of NSA comes to about 5.68 only. The pressure of man on land is very high. The per capita share of area in Vaishali is (0.09) hectare whiles the corresponding figure for Bihar and India are (0.219) hectare and (0.39) hectare respectively.

198 lakh hectares of land of Vaishali district is cropped out of this only 0.80 lakh hectares is irrigated. Thus only about 40% of the cropped area of the district is irrigated. Thus, the present, situation in Vaishali district displays that Agricultural efficiency in every part of the region is not satisfactory. This can be brought upto the mark by providing modern infrastructural facilities improved seeds. Improved farming techniques such as use of fertilizers, mechanical

inputs tractors, power tillers, threshers, irrigation facilities etc. Above all the productivity of land can be increased by the uplifting the socio-economic conditions of the farmers.

Carrying Capacity of Land :

The term carrying capacity refers to the maximum number or people that a given land area will maintain in perpetuity under a given system of uses without land degradation settings. Stamp has raised two important questions, the first is the maximum number of people which a square mile of productive land can support in terms of food and the second is the population needed to secure maximum production with maximum efficiency.

Scholars have tried to assess the productive capacity of land an its mind bearing capacity. Mukherjee is of the opinion that in a country like India one acre of agricultural land would be indispensable for the nourishment of one person. Shafi is more optimistic when he highlights the capacity of agricultural land of India to bear the burden of five times the existing population. The carrying capacity of land depends upon the nature of land available. The lands of the area under study Vaishali district are very fertile. One the basis of fertility these are divided into bhit land, Dhanhar land, gaurha land etc. It has been found that gaurha land bhit land and dhanhar land have different carrying capacity. The gaurha land can support 5-6 persons is an acre of land as they are most fertile land. While bhit land and Dhanhar land can support 3 persons.

A farmer having one acre of good quality is considered more prosperous than a farmer who owns two or three acres of unproductive land. Table 5.4 shows the carrying capacity of one hectare of agricultural land in the region.

It is observed from the table that the land of Vaishali is so intensively used that seems to be little possibilities of increasing the productions and the carrying capacities of the land. The pressure of population is very high. The per capita land available in Vaishali district is (0.09 hectare/person) while it is (0.219 hectare) in Bihar and (0.39 hectares) in India.

Table 5.4
Carrying Capacity of one hectare in land in Vaishali

Type of land Cropping	Intensity of Crop	Principal	Yield in kg. capacity	Carrying
1. Good quality land	Very high	Bhadai Maize " Paddy " Marua Aghani Paddy " Wheat " Potato Garma Paddy " Maize " Vegetable Bhadai Paddy " Maize " Marua " Arhar Aghani Paddy	High 2000-3000 kg.	15
2. Medium high quality land	High	Rabi wheat " Gram " Khesari " oil seeds Garma Paddy " Maize	Moderate 1500-2000 kg.	10
3. Poor quality land	Low	Aghani paddy	Low 1000-2000 kg.	8

Source : Self computed by the authors on datas available.

References :

1. Mukherjee, R.K. (1933) : The Changing face of Bengal : A study in Rural economy, Calcutta, p. 239.
2. Hunter, M.W. (1877) : Statistical Account of Bengal, Vol. XIII, p. 111.
3. Zimmerman, EW (1933) : Worlds resources Industries, pp. 82-100.
4. Mukherjee, A.B. : Spatial patterns of multiple cropping in India, Essays on Agricultural Geography 1959, p. 159s.

5. Hussain, M. (1979) : Agricultural geography, p. 114.
6. Singh, Jasbir : Agricultural geography Tata Mcgraw Hill Publishing Company Ltd. 1982.
7. Whittlsey Derment : Major agricultural regions of the earth, annals of the association of American Geographers (1936), p. 209.
8. Kawachi, Kamichi : On apex method of classifying world agricultural region – Tokyo, Proceedings of IGU, Regional Conference in Japan 1957.
9. Kostorwicky, Jersy : Geographical typology of agriculture principles and methods, Geographia, Polonica (1964), pp. 111-146.
10. Buchanan, R.O. : Some reflections on agricultural geography. Geography (1959), pp. 1-13.
11. Singh, Jasbir : An agricultural Geography of India–A Geographical analysis of Kurukshetra, Vishal Publication (1974), p. 1.
12. Simons, L. (1967) : Agricultural Geography.
13. Vink, A.P.A. (1976) : Land use in Advancing agriculture springer and verlague, Germany p. 18.
14. Shafi, M. (1969) : Can India support Five times of its population?" Science today, p. 24.
15. Withelmy, H. (1973) : Studies in Rices cultivations in S.E. Asia Applied Science and Development. Vol.2, p. 65.

6

Growth Centres

Development is a dynamic concept. Development has been defined as "a process of growth, expansion or realization of potential bringing regional resources into full productive use. " There has always been discussion over the centralized model of development and decentralized model. The general tendency in most developing countries is to centralize the power of decision making. The advocates of decentralization are however, not convinceds of this, and would like a structures wherein the central authority has only a limitd role to play.

Although in a democracy like ours all sectors of the economy is so interlinked and inter dependent that it is very difficult to lift up one region neglecting the others. The advocate of centralized development found the growth pole or growth centre theory a handy tool to rationalize their stand. The adherents of the growth centre and Industrial fundamentalism were convinced that was essentially spot based. It could not be started everywhere, given the limitation of resources and hence must be promoted in selected sectors and places.

Growth Centres – a technique in area development :

Growth centre, model of development process has been the rallying point for many of the growth economists and almost every developing country opted for the Growth centre approach toward development during the 1960.

India after independence embarked upon a centralized plan for the development of the country. The economic planners who believe in the Growth centre theory of the development feel that in due course of time the growth impluses could move to the remaining sectors and areas leading ultimatly to the development of all the sectors and regions. They believe in what is popularly known as the "trickle-down process" of development. During the fifties and sixties, planners and policy-makers considered rural areas to be traditional; they thought they would disapper as the urban developmental centres would engulfed them. The tendency to make central authorities strong is visible since long times all over the world – both in developed and developing countries. Many states or even civilizations have withered away in the past only because the central authorities were weak. A Strong and healthy state invariably needs a strong central authority interlinked with dispersed growth centres for a balance growth. "Development from above or below?" is controversy still continued. The inablity of most developing countries to generate rapid growth to remove mass poverty, led many a theorist to believe that it was because of the failure of central or Top-down planning and development to penetrate into the rural areas. Hence the theory of Growth centre prove to be the best suitable technique for the development of a region.

In which there is a harmonious relationship between the centre and states, or regions. The region under study Vaishali centre prove to be the best suitable technique for the development of a region.

(1) Vaishali :

This anchal is in the Northern part of the district. The district derives its name from this anchal. It is an ancient place of spiritual importance from Hindus, Jaina and Buddhists. It is being developed as a big tourist spot. Its total area is 132 km^2 with a population of 146 lakh. Literacy rate is 41% main crops of the anchal are paddy, wheat, fruits and vegetables and pulses. This anchal is free from flood as it is situated on high level. Soils are also rich. So this has a vast potential for agrobased industries. Roads and Transport facilities are needed to be developed so that this anchal could be on international tourist destination.

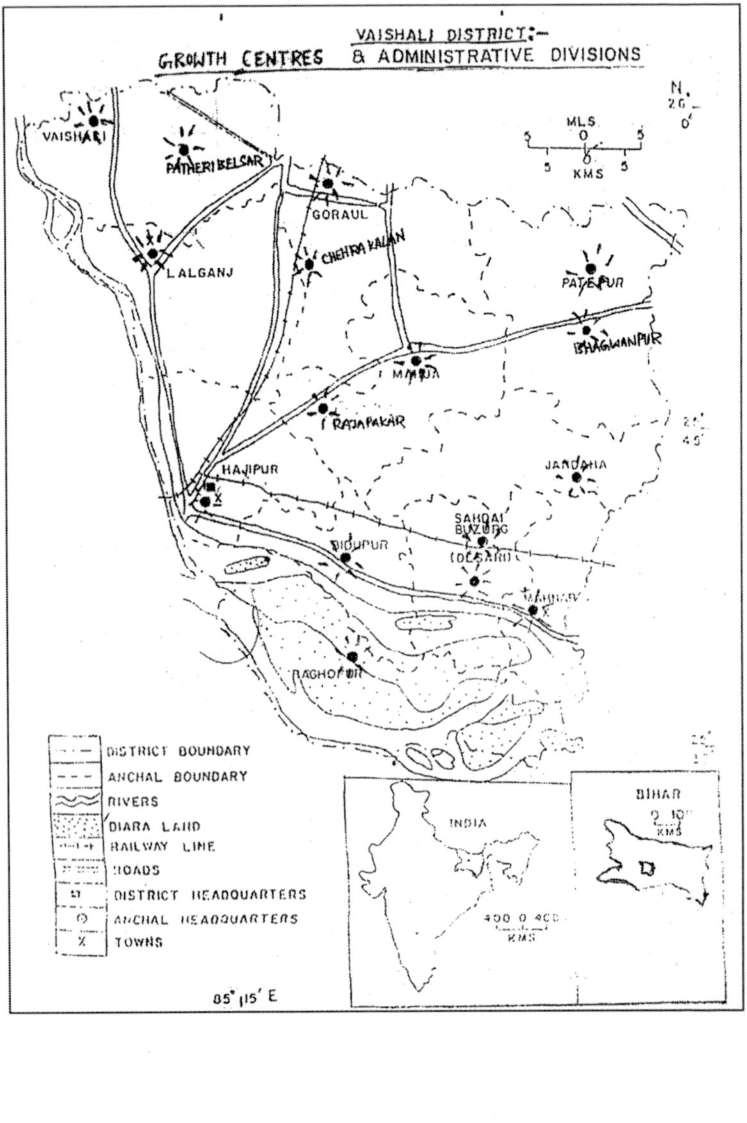
VAISHALI DISTRICT:-
GROWTH CENTRES & ADMINISTRATIVE DIVISIONS
VAISHALI
PATHERI BELSAR
LALGANJ
GORAUL
CHEHRA KALAN
PATEPUR
BHAGWANPUR
RAJAPAKAR
HAJIPUR
JANDAHA
SAHDAI BUZURG
(DESARI)
BIDUPUR
RAGHOPUR
MLS
KMS
DISTRICT BOUNDARY
ANCHAL BOUNDARY
RIVERS
DIARA LAND
RAILWAY LINE
ROADS
DISTRICT HEADQUARTERS
ANCHAL HEADQUARTERS
TOWNS
INDIA
BIHAR
85° 15' E

Fig. 6.1

(2) Patheri Belsar :

This new anchal is in Northern part of the district. Its total area is 74.16 km^2 and population is 0.74 lakh. Most of the people involved in cultivation literacy rate is 37.5%. Major crops are wheat, paddy and pulses. Agrobased industries would also flourish in this anchal, but communication and tranport facility must improve. For the human resource development more High Schools, Colleges and Hospitals are needed.

(3) Lalganj :

This anchal is located in northern part. Its total area is 151 km^2 with headquarter through NH31. Major crops of this anchal are wheat, pulses, sugarcane, tobacco etc. This anchal is connected by the National Highway. Sugar mills and potato chips making units could run well here.

(4) Bhagwanpur :

This anchal is situated in the central part. Total area is 118.28 km^2 and population 1.62 lakh literacy is 42%. Major are wheat, paddy, oilseeds, sugarcane, maize etc. This anchal needs 2 high schools and one degree college so that educations is promoted in this anchal. There is also need for the development of Transportation facilties.

(5) Goraul :

This anchal is in central part of the district. Total area is 98.88 km^2 and population 1.40 lakh literacy rate is 32%. It is very important agricultural region. Main crops are sugarcane, paddy, wheat, banana etc. Here some sugar mills and agrobased are also established. But more of them need to be established here as there is plenty of agricultural products in this anchal.

(6) Chehra Kalan :

This new anchal is in central part of the district. Its total area is 68.31 km^2 with a population of 1.02 lakh. Literacy rate is 36% main crops are paddy, wheat, pulses, mung etc. Agrobased industries are not developed. Some gur making units and rice mills, and furniture making units are running in this anchal. Lack of communication system and electric supply are hindrances in the way of establishing big units.

(7) Patepur :

This anchal is situated in the North eastern part. It has an area of 256.57 km^2 its population is 2.82 lakh. Literacy rate is 34%. This anchal is mainly producer of paddy, wheat, pulse and oilseeds. In rural areas dairy farming and fishing is practised as there is vast grazing lands available in this anchal known as 'chaurs'. 'Tal baraila' is the biggest chaur of the district. There is lack of educational institutions such as schools and colleges. These institution must be established to make this anchal strong in human resource development.

(8) Mahua :

This anchal is situated in the central part. It's area extends upto 140.30 km^2. Its population is 2.18 lakh. Literacy rate is 40%. Its main agricultural productss are Banana, Sugarcane, Paddy, Wheat and Pulse. There is one sugar mill, few small leather extracting units and gur making units in this anchal. There is need for two high school, one college and one big referal hospital in this anchal for proper health and education facility in this anchal.

(9) Jandaha :

This anchal is in East central part. Its area is 150.32 km^2 and population 2.07 lakh. Literacy rate is 40.50%. Main products are, wheat, maize, paddy, pulse, Banana, vegetables etc. Some parts of this anchal are water logged during rainy season. Transport and communication facilities are in the poor state in this anchal.

(10)Raja Pakar :

This anchal is in central part. Total area is 75.57 km^2 & Population is 1.20 lakh. Literacy rate is 41.56%. Paddy and wheat are the main agricultural product. Banana and Mango orchards are also found in this anchal. Due to vicinity of the district headquarter Hajipur this anchal has a great potential for development of agro industries, factories and farm lands. There is need to Transportation facilties and good electricity supply so that this anchal could become a growth centre in true sense of the word. There is also scarcity of goods educational institutes for higher education.

(11)Hajipur :

It is most important anchal of the district. The administrative headquarter of the district is located here. This anchal is the most developed anchal of the district. The zonal headquarter of the East Central railways is located here. It extends upto an area of 156.86 km^2. Its population is 3.49 lakh. Literacy rate is 47%. It is well connceted with other parts of the country through Water transport, Road transport and Railways. Educational Institutes, Hotel Management Institute, Big hospitals has been established and more such Institutes are in the process. Big colonies and markets are also being built here. Land prices have increased four folds during 10 years. This is due to the vicinity of the state capital Patna. This anchal has also been incorporated in the proposed greater Patna project. This is the most rapidly growing anchal of Vaishali district.

(12)Raghopur :

It is the Southern anchal of the district. Its total area is 225.80 km^2 and population 1.87 lakh. Literacy rate is 26.20%. This is the most backward anchal of the district. Annual flood is the main feature of its climate due to its law lying fields. Main crops of the anchals are Maize, wheat, paddy, banana and vegetables. River transport is developed in the anchal. It is well connected with state capital Patna through river Ganga. There is scarcity of road transport or railways in this anchal. This is a flood prone area and almost six months a year most of its areas are water logged. There is vast potentiality in this anchal for vegetable production, sand extraction and fishing.

(13)Bidupur :

It is situated in the southern part. Its area is 114.54 km^2 and population 2.07 lakh. Literacy rate is 43%. Main crops of this anchal are wheat, paddy, maize, fruits, vegetables and pulses. People practice four to five crops combinations because of the fertility of the soil and good irrigational facilties. There is need for big cold storage and good quality roads in this anchal so that all its products are preserved and sent to big markets.

(14)Desri :

This anchal is situated in the south eastern part. Its areas extends upto 49.99 km^2. Its population is 0.77s lakh. Literacy rate is 40%. This anchal has is also rich in fertile soil. Four crop combination is practiced here. They are wheat, paddy, maize, fruits and vegetables. There is need of one degree college and two +2 level schools for educating youth of this anchals. One cold storage is being established. This will be very beneficial for the farmers of the anchal.

(15)Sahdai Bujurg :

This anchal is in south eastern part. Its area is 87.74 km^2 and population 0.97 lakh. Literacy rate is 41%. Paddy is the main crop of this anchal but wheat, oilseed and pulse are also cultivated. This anchal is also big producer of sugarcane but there is no sugar mill around so most of the product is wasted. Agrobased industries could develop here if government provided support.

(16)Mahnar :

This anchal is in South eastern part of the district. Its total area is 89.87 km^2 and its total population is 1.43 lakh. Its literacy rate is 41%. There is one college and 2 High school in this anchal. There is need for at least one more college and 2 more High schools in this anchal. Roads of state government are in good shape. Some parts of this anchal is waterlogged during rainy season. These wastelands could be used for producing souft word and pisciculture.

Concept of Growth Centre :

Developments is a complex process : It is a process of change in the socio-economic status of the society. There has been two streams of thought over the development process. One group of the Geographer feel that development process should take place from the top to bottom. They thought centralized planning was essential for the development of a region. While advocates of other view believed that developmental process should begin at the region itself.

The geographers who supported the centralized planning found the growth pole theory a handy tool to rationalize their stand. The growth pole or growth centre theory is based on the Idea that development could not be started everywhere because of the limitations of availabilities of physical as well as socio-economic resources. The planners should concentrate on the selected sectors for growth activities. In today capitalist society, vast concentrations of capital, and labour come together in an area to form a complex system where information and ideas as well as material goods and even labour power more around with relative case.

This situation leads towards development process with the establishment of factories, schools, roads, churches, temples, shopping centres, parks, hospitals and railways facilities in an area. The are later transforms into a growth centre. Growth centre is invariably the result of capitalist economy with the support of Industrialisation in the 18th century the Growth centres developed on a large scale. Small towns developed at the site of Minning areas. Ship harbours, markets, railways junctions, production units, all leading to the development of Growth centres.

Although the concept of growth centre is not new but it got concrete shape in the sixties, when many geographers gave their hypobook over growth centre viz – core peripheri model, Rostow's model, central business district model etc.

In the core-peripheri model a central part dominates in

the concentration of economic power, technical progress and productive activities while the peripheri is dependent. Core-Peripheri model is most closely associated with the hypobook of John Friedmann (1966). The spatial arrangement and tranformation of a capitalist economy at a particular point reflects above all the current requirements of accumulation and the historical legacy of landscape created by previous rounds of accumulation of resources.

In this way the concentration of control is more likely to be intensified rather the reduced as the economy becoem highly integrated in spatial terms and geographical development evolves in accordance with a developments plan. The American economist W.W. Rostow (1971) postulated a sequence of economic growth in a region. His projection for economic development was based on two factors, First, the region could develop if the technical skill and human resources used judiciously. He gives example of Japan. It Japan could develop why not other countries? Second, many less developed regions contained an abundant supply of raw materials which could be used to generate the take-off stage in economic development. The most suitable is oil rich middle east.

The theory of central Business District (CBD) depicts every growth centre or, old city has the core; which is characterized by intensive land development, tall buildings, many stores and offices and crowded streets. Just outside the core is the frame or Fringe of the CBD, this is an area of wholeselling activities, transportation terminals, warehouses, new car dealers, furnitures stores, recreation terminals, Warehouses, new car dealers, furniture stores, recreation centres and even light Industries. Just beyond the (CBD) is the beginning of residential land uses. Around the CBD is usually transition zone in which a number of land uses are found. Some setions of this zone may be occupied by older buildings which will gradually be replaced by the growth of the CBD or by change to one of the other transitional functions, such as filling stations car sales rooms, super markets, boarding houses, hotels and some other industrial activity. Such uses reflect and the cost of land. The next zone is that of working class housing and industry. This area was once, perhaps one of better class housing but age and the growth of traffic and the urban problems have lowered its status. This zone in inhabited by working class people who cannot afford to move out to better homes in the middle class residential districts. New suburban areas are inhabited by middle class to wealthy citizens. The suburbs grade into a computer belt where old villages or towns and modern housing development are occupied by people who travel each day to offices in the city centre. Between the suburbs there may be stretches of agricultural land. This land is devoted to the most profitable forms of farming namely, market gardening dairy farming and intensive poultry farming and provides the city with fresh vegetables, fruits, milk etc. All these factors combine to produce a pattern of zones which is relatively unrealted to strictly economic factors, but which reflects the piecemeal development and expansion of towns by different people or for specific reasons.

Methodology :

In the present work an attempt has been made to study and analyse the pattern of development of Growth centres. The census of 1991 and 2001 has been selected for the data analysis at block levels. These datas were made available from the department of statistics and evaluation, Government of Bihar, Patna. Extensive tour was done by the candidate to get on the spot verification of the facts and figures. Special attempt has been made to emphasise the agricutlural features as well as geographical factors. Because Agriculture is the main resource of the development of rural economy. Besides this, stress has been given to discuss infrastructures for development of agriculture and agro-based industries, cottage industries, institutions for human resource development. Role of communication and media is also studies for proper evaluation of growth centres. All these facts have been studied after physical verification questionnaires filled up by local people.

References :

1. Hussain, M. (1994) : Human Geography, Rawat Publication, New Delhi.
2. Singh, R.P. (2007) : Rural development and Panchayati Raj in India, Janaki Prakashan, Patna.
3. Chatterjee, S.P. (1941) : "The place of Geography in national planning" Calcutta Geographical, Patna.
4. Singh, R.L. (1960) : Geographical concepts and methods of research work, National Geographical society of India Varanasi, Vol. VI, part 3, p. 135.
5. Provisional Population totals census of India 2001, series 11, Bihar, p. 27.
6. District census handbook of Vaishali 1991 and 2001.
7. Singh, R.P. and Kumar, Anil (1970) : "Monograph of Bihar" Bharati Bhawan Publication, Patna.
8. Singh, R.L. (1960) : India – A regional Geography, N.G.S.I., Varanasi, p. 28.

7

Rural Area Development

After Independence India embarked upon comprehensive national development and in this endeavour rural development has got preponderance because of the fact that overwhelming population of India live in villages and all round problems there, are not only patheric but also rural development national development will simply be fatuous. Nearly 75% of the total population of our country resides in villages. Nearly four out of five persons in our country reside in rural areas. Almost 75% of people are involved in Agriculture directly or indirectly. India is an agricultural economy where agriculture contibutes 50% of the National income. Despite the fact, there is a wide gap between the rural India and urban India. This gap is not only economic but also socio-cultural.

Bases of Rural Development :

Problems of the rural areas have recently been viewed more and moe in terms of what they mean to people because India as the second largest populated country of the world and its greatest resource is people. As said by Whipple "A nation's true wealth lies not in its lands and water, not in forests and mines, not in flocks and herds, not in its dollars but lies in its healthy men, women and children."

A planned approach to the Utilization of human resources in needed for an integrated rural development of the district. Vaishali is a backward district of Bihar where social inequality, physical and economic exploitation of people is prevelent. In the sociological analysis of poverty inequality and backwardness of the developed section of the region it is found that social and economic handicap is rooted in the social inequality and caste hierarchy. These have rendered certain group of society severly disadvantaged.

Besides that Infrastructural facilities for the rural development such as Electricity Communication roads, schools, health facilities are also absent. Unemployment, illiteracy, landlessness untouchability and high pressure of population on agriculture are bane to rural development of the region. Thus, bases for rural development could be grouped under two segments.

(a) Economic development.

(b) Socio-Cultural development

(a) Economic development : Economic Development calls for employment generation through Agro based industries, village cottage industries, Agricultural reform and agricultural efficiency.

(b) Socio-cultural development : Human resources development through literacy, health facilities to all families, family planning and caster stigma should be abolished.

Potentiality of Rural Development

India is on a threshold of historic transition of political and economic process to the grassroots. Its economic upshots can hardly be overlooked. The decentralization process initiated since independence has incorporated many important policy strategies for accelerating rural development in the country. Needless to emphasise that in predominantly agricultural country where 75% of the population reside in rural areas and more than one third of the total workforce are engaged in a agriculture and its allied activities. The policy strategy has always remained on giving more accent on the development of the rural economy. Gandhi's dream of 'Gram Swaraj' was also a manifestation of rural development. The aim of Gram Swaraj was also to uplift the people particularly the rural from the syndrome of low-socio economic development.

Acharya Vinova Bhave was of the opinion that imbalance of land distribution in rural was responsible for the poverty in villages. Community development programme and National Extension service were introduced during first five year plan to upbring positive changes in the socio-cultural life of villages introduced five year plans and 20 point programmes thrust was on the rural development, but despite the commendable objectives, these programmes could not unleash transformation of the rurals economy. In fact from the policy strategy point of view, decentralization was supposed to be a panacea for rural development. The Panchayati raj system was then applied in villages through 73rd amendment of the constitution. It was believed that central administration and economic aid was not enough villagers could solve their economic and social problems themselves if they are provided with necessary powers.

Vaishali district is a fully agriculture oriented region endowed with rich fertile soil and water resources. Again it has vast human resource enriched by a cultural heritage. Yet the region is one of the poorest and most underdeveloped part of the country. The region reflects, in essence, all the problems of under development in the country in an acute form, though its economy, which has to be essentially agricultural and agro-industrial, can be made viable and healthy. The region is endowed with a vast well drained and almost isotropic land with one of the richest soil cover. Still, the region suffers from droughts and floods almost alternatively and these could easily remedied by the introduction of a well articulated irrigation cum drainage system and reafforestation and land management system. Man is the creator of all forms of wealth. Vaishali has enough of manpower but this manpower is not properly utilized. 80% of the people are directly or indirectly involved in agriculture for their livelihood. It is evident that pressure of man on land is immense. This is the main reason of low productivity and heavy consumption of food grains in the area. The density of population is also very high 1332 while it is 880 for Bihar and 324 for India. This human resource could be well absorbed in agro-based industries and food processing industries. Vaishali is famous for Banana, guava, lichi, Mango, sugarcane and vegetable production. Sugar factories, Dairy farming, poultry farming, piggery are some of the small scale industries which would flourish in the area. Other problems in agricultural sector are low productivity, subsistence farming, flood and drought, unavailability of irrigation facilities. Lack of scientific knowledge and proper marketing facilties for their agricultural products.

Education is the most important component of human resource development. The region is very backward in the literacy rate. The literacy rate for men 48% and women 32% is far less than those of Bihar and India. Vaishali District Male literacy 75.41%, Female literacy 56.73% (Census 2011). The network of educational facilities in the area is very poor. There are 16 colleges, 142 high schools and 1500 primary schools while the district has a population of 27,12,389. According to the Bye laws 1976 of planning commission of Bihar government, there should be a degree college on 75000-100000 persons, a high school for 15000 persons and a primary school for 2000 persons. On these standards there is a huge gap between the requirement and supply of the educational institution. There should be establishment of educational institutions at the rate of growing population to meet the demand.

Transport and communication is as important for the development of a region as circulation of blood for human body. Vaishali district is serveds by only 26% of the villages with pucca roads. All important places and anchal headquarters are connected through a network of all weather roads. But the interior villages are devoid of this facility. If villages are provided with pucca roads this would help in the transportation of men and materials, thereby helping the development of the region. Health is an entry point for all development activities to be planned and organized by the community. That is why, the provision of sufficient medical and health services is an item of best investment. In Vaishali district health services are provided through private hospitals, dispensaries and health centres but the number of these institutions are not satisfactory. It is suggested that an additional 23 hospitals should be established in the district to meet the demand of the people. If above sectors are analysed by the government and met with proper arrangement for the supply of the neccesary aid then, no doubt the district could be one of the most developed in the country.

Plan of rural Development

The paradigm of developments theory has recently undergone a revolutionary change. Development is new regarded as a process that requires proper planning. The concept of development has come a long way from mere economic growth of growth with equity and justice, from governmental initiative to people's participation and involvement. from socio-economic development to human resource development and from endowment empowerment. It is now realized and avowed that development of rural India can be concrete only through the process of decentralized planning and implementation fully. To achieve fast growth of economy and uplift living standard of people India embarked upon systematic plan.

Planning in one form or, another can not be dispensed with by any societies aspiring to raise the standards of living of its members. The very fact that almost all countries of the world have now adopted planning as a technique for socio-economic development is a fair indication of its crucial role. Any plan is resorted to for a variety of purpose – economic growth, social welfare, human resources developments etc. Thus, there are two basic elements or dimensions of a plan These are (a) Economic development, (b) Social development. Vaishali district's main economic work is agriculture. 80% of its population is involved in agricultural activity.

Literacy rate is very low, unemployment and social stigma

of casteism is high. A systematic plan for the development of district could be grouped under the following heads :

1. Plan for agricultural development
2. Plan for the development of socio-economic infrastructure.
3. Plan related to population pressure
4. Plan for Industrial development

1. **Plan for Agricultural development :** The are many problems in agriculture in the district viz. Heavy pressure of population on land, unequal distribution of land dependence on Monsoon for irrigation, obsolete techinque of agriculture etc. These problems could be sorted out by the use of high yielding seeds, New improved techinque and machinery such as, tractors, harvesters etc. use of fertilizers, pesticides, irrigation by pumpsets etc.

2. **Plan for the development of socio-economic infrastructure :** Economic growth without social development is possible only at the cost of common man's values. Socio-economic development means optimum utlizations of qualities and resources of the poeple. The important social infrastructure are the facilities of education, medical, communication, drinking water, housing etc.

Literacy rate of the district is very low. This could be attributed to the poor network of education institutions. The district has a population of 27,12,389 persons. Cater to the need of the people there are only 16 colleges. 142 High schools and 1500 Primary schools in the district. Keeping in view the Bihar government's planning standards there should be at least 35 colleges, 192 high school and 1636 primary schools in the district.

Development of Transport and communication system is needed for the sucess of social development programmes. Only 26% people of the district are served by pucca roads.

Except anchal headquarter and city areas interior villages are devoid of pucca approach road. It is suggested that all village kutcha roads be converted into pucca metallic roads to make them operative in rainy season. This will help in the transportation of men and materials, thereby helping the development of human resources. The existing postal and communication services in the district is not satisfactory. Only about 14% villages are served by post and telegraph offices. There are 174 post offices and 19 telegraph offices in the district. The number of post offices required more in the Hajipur anchal is (4), Lalganj (5), Mahua (1) and Raghopur (1) 2. additional telegraph offices should be established in Hajipur, Mahua and Raghopur each and 1 in Goraul, Patepur and Jandaha respectively.

In Vaishali health services are provided through Primary health centre (PHC), Primary health sub centres Maternity and Child Welfare Centres (MCWC) and Family Palnning Centres (FPC). But the number and functioning of these medical institutions are not satisfactory. These are also not distributed evenly in the district. It is suggested that an additional 23 hospitals should be establisheds in the dsitrict. As Goraul, Sahdai Bujurg, and Raghopur do not have hospital, one each should be established at anchal headquarters. 18 more health centre of different nature are proposed to be established in the district.

3. **Planning related to population pressure** : The area under study shows heavy pressure on land. The density of the area is 1332. Cause for this phenomena are low marriage age (child marriage), Agricultural society joint family where childrens are joint responsibility, illiteracy, religious beliefs and hot weather condition. This could be checked by bring down birth rate raise the marrigable age, advertisement of family planning measures in villages, Education through print, Radio and TV media, Family control programme measures should be easily available at all medical stores, government health centres.

4. **Planning for Industrial development :** The district is

backward in industrial development due to lack of basic raw materials. But the region is very fertile and suitable for Agro-based industries. Hajipur Industrial estate may be developed and industrial units related to juice making, banana chips making, agricultural tools making and others depeneding upon the local demand may be established. Agro based industries such as Rice mills, Flour, frills, oil mills, gur making be established in every village. Other cottage industries could be poultry, dairy, furniture making iron grills making etc.

Thus on the basis of research made so far it can be remarked that the upliftment or, development of the rural areas of the district could be based upon agriculture and agro-based industries. Financial assistance from the government to the enterpreneurs be provided for establishing cold storage chains where perishable items such as eggs, vegetables fruits etc could be stored.

Illustration of Rural Development :

The Vaishali district is a part of middle Ganga plain and primarily derives its resources from the rich fertile soils, and water resources of the vast plain. It has immense human resources enriched by a cultural heritage of millennia of years. Yet the region is one of the poorest and under developed parts of the country. Though the district's economy is based upon agriculture. It is dependent mostly on Monsoonal rain. Pressure of population on land is very high. On the social front, there is high growth of popualtions rate, illiteracy and unemployment is rampant.

If the rural development scenario of the region is illustrated, it could be grouped under following heads :

(a) Demographic features

(b) Agricultural land use pattern

(c) Socio-economic infrastructure

(d) Industrial development

(a) **Demographic features :** Vaishali district is highly population in the Bihar plain. In year 1951 the growth rate of population was 19.05% while in 2001 it is 29.08%. The enormous growth rate of population has resulted due to high birth rate and low death rate. The death rate decreased during 50 years rapidly because of the latest medical facilities were available and epidemic death due to cholera, plague, small pox and diarrhea controlled by the governmental effort other reasons could be low marriage age, illiteracy, social beliefs agricultural economy etc.

According to 2001 census Hajipur is the most densely populated anchal of the district while Raghopur has lowest density of population. The central part of the district is highly populated. Northern and North-Western part is moderately populated while the southern part of the district is low populated. Literacy rate of the region is lower 40.82%, than the state 47.53% and the country 64.80%, it is indicator of the low level of human resource development in the district. Literacy rate varies from anchal to anchal. Hajipur is the most literate 50.16% anchal while Raghopur 26.02% is the poorest of all.

The occupational structure of the region determines whether the economy is agricultural, industrial or semi industrial. In Vaishali district highest number of workers are engaged in agricultural activities. They are cultivators or farmers and agricultural labourers. Cultivators constitute 49% of the main workers and agricultural labourers are 38% of the main workers. Other workers are engaged in household industries such as animal husbandry pottery, masonary etc. The above facts shows that about 86% of the main workers of Vaishali are agriculturists.

(b) **Agricultural landuse pattern :** The landuse pattern of Vaishali is uneven. Some parts of district contain higher ground, some contain lower ground, while some are fertile and others it is not so. These factors have made very differences in the intensity of cropping crop combination and land use pattern in different anchals. Patepur, Lalganj and Vaishali rank high in the New sown area where it ranges from 70%-82% of the Arable land. While Hajipur, Bidupur and Sahdai Bujurg are poor in net sown area (60%-65%).

There are four agricultural season in the district namely. Bhadai, Aghani, Rabi and Garma. Of these Aghani (Kharif) and Rabi season is most important as during these seasons two important food grains of the region paddy and wheat is grown.

The Rabi crop occupies maximum land about 76,229 hectares. Aghani crops occupy 58.311 hectares Garma 40,525 hectares and Bhadai 23092 hectares respectively. In this way rabi crop in the most significant accounting for 38.98% of the total cropped area. Vaishali district's all anchals have very high index of intensity of cropping. The highest figure is recorded by Sahdai Bujurg (172%) followed by Mahua and Lalganj (164%) each. On the other hand, Agriculture is mostly done on natural supply of water during monsoon. There is heavy pressure of man on agricultural land, commercial crops are cultivated in limited areas, fertilizers are (10.4kg) meagerly used. These are some of the problems of agriculture in Vaishali district.

(c) **Socio-economic Infrastructure :** Social development can be defined as the optimum utilization of qualities and resources of the people and for the balanced developed of people and the country. The perameters of socio-economic development of a region could be facilities available to the people in terms of Nutrition, housing, clothing, water supply, sanitary condition, health facilities, education and transportation facilities. On the above parameters Vaishali is a backward district. The literacy rate of male 48.98% and female is 32.02%. It is due to poor network of educational institution in the region. Hajipur 50.16% is the most literate anchal while Raghopur 26.02% is poor. Only about 26% of the villages are served by metalled road most of them become in operative during rainy season due to flood. Vaishali is served by East-central railway with its headquarter at Hajipur. But almost 90% of the railway lines are single track taking enormous time in transportation. River tranport is used in river side areas. Raghopur is connected with Patna and other parts of the Vaishali district through river.

(d) **Industrial development :** The existing industry of the study areas may be classified into two types as large scale industry and cottage small scale industry. The traditional cottage industries like biri making, earthen pottery, shoes making, basket making, blanket making etc. are still carried on but they are mostly locally marketed and the people employed in these are mostly low caste. Small scale industries include Rice mills, sugar mills flour mills, gur making, wooden furniture and soap making etc. The government under 20 point programmes and the district Industrial department are encouraging these industries by providing subsidies, seeds, money and credit facilities on easy terms which has greatly helped the rural artisans in improving their lots. Punjab National Bank and State Bank of India have been specially entrusteds with the responsibility of providing financial assistance to rural entrepreneurs.

Due to lack of basic raw materials Vaishali is poor in Industrial development. There is no large scale industry in the region. There is a sugar factory at Goraul, a few tobacco making factories are located at Mahnar. Mahesh glass factory at Hajipur is the main glass factory which manufactures Bangles, Jars, tumblers, and other articles. The prospect of industrialization of the district has improved immensely due to the opening of the ganga bridge. An industrial estate has been established at Hajipur in which nearly 50 industries have been set up.

Projection of rural development :

India has been Familiar with the concept of social and

economic planning for a long time. As early as 1876 Dada bhai Naoroji wrote a paper on poverty in India asserting that poverty under the raj was increasing and demanding organized remedial procedures, planning under a democratic system, may be defined as the technical co-ordination, of consumption, production, investment, trade and income distributions in accordance with social objectives. Such planning is not only to be considered from the point of view of economics, and the raising of the standard of living; but must include cultural and spiritual values, and the human side of life. One of the earliest actions of the independent India's government was to set up planning commission. To achieve fast growth of economy and uplift the living standard of any region a well planned developments process has to be embarked upon. The area under study Vaishali district is primarily an agro based economy and it is in the secondary phase of development. The level of education and standards of living in rurals areas is very low, they are backward from all points of view.

The project of developments for the district must address the propers utilization of its natural resources viz. Fertile soil, water resources as well as its human resource like availability of vast population. This project could be grouped under the following heads :

(i) Projection of agricultural development

(ii) Projection of Socio-economics infrastructure

(iii) Projection of Human resource development

(iv) Projection of Industrial development

(i) Projection of Agricultural Development : The landuse pattern of Vaishali is not uniform due to its geographical situtation. Nothern parts have higher ground while southern and eastern parts are lower, which are inundated flood almost every year, and are left unused for many months.

These areas could be a best utilized by fish cultivations in small ponds. Some farmers may do combined cultivation of fish and rice. Farmers are encouraged by Bihar government for fisheries through subsidized seeds, feed and loan for the management and maintenance of such ponds. Other problems of agriculture are low productivity, heavy pressure of man on land and dependence on Monsoonal rain for irrigation. These problems could be sorted out through irrigation by private pumpsets, use of hybrid seds which yieds more harvest and takes less time for ripening use of latest machines in agriculture. These are available through banks easy loan schemes and kisan credit cards. Vaishali is rich in fruits and vegetable production, but due to lack of proper network of marketing and agro based industries major part of the production is degraded. Market must be established in every block where locals would sell their vegetables, milk and eggs. A chain of cold storage in the district. There in Hajipur Anchal in Goraul, one in Lalganj, one in Vaishali and one in Mahnar anchal. Viewing the need of the district at least (12) more cold storages should be built. Besides, that, food processing industries could be established at Hajipur Industrial development authority premises out of the agricultural land only 64% is sown with crops out of the rest 12.62% is Barren and uncultivable waste land, fallow land cover about. 4% which may be brought under plough by providing irrigation, fertillizer etc. Vaishali is rich in livestock still it has good potential for milk production. This can be done by scientific cattle rearing organized on commercial basis. Two programmes have been under taken by the government in this direction. The first is Mini dairy scheme under which farmers are provided with Five crops breed cows the second is the Integrated Rural Development Programme in which government provides assistances to marginal and small farmers. At present there is neither any government cattle farm nor poultry farm in the district. So there should be at least (5) five poultry farm and five (5) Cattle farm established by the government.

(ii) **Projection of Socioeconomic infrastructure :** Economic growths without social development is possible only at the cost of common man's value. The development projection of developing countries should be so articulated that it does not only promote economic growth but also social development. Social development can also be defined as the optimum utilization of qualities and resources of the people and for the balanced development of the people and of the study area.

Any region is developed or underdeveloped in proportion to the qualities and standards of human resources and it will progressively be instrumental in creating opportunities for all inhabitants on an equitable basis for their self realization at appropriate locations. The UNICEF has provided a model of social inputs and the components included in it are called 'WHENEERS'.

W - Water for drinking and household use

H - Health care, preventive, promotive as well as curative

E - Education to children, women and men

N - Nutrition, adequate for growth, play and work

E - Economic activities especially for women

R - Recreations especially for children

S - Shelter for healthy living.

Education :

It is the most important component of human resources development. In Vaishali district only 40% people are literate. The literacy percentage among men and women are 48% and 32% respectively. This show the backwardness of the study area. The network of educational institution is very poor. There are 16 colleges 142 high schools and 1500 primary schools in the district. Keeping view of the Bihar Government's planning standards there should be 19 colleges, 50 high school and 136 more primary schools required in the area.

Hajipur does not need additional college. Lalganj, Bidupur and Raghopur need one more college each. Two new colleges are needed by the anchals of Vaishali, Mahua,

Jandaha, Mahnar, Sahdai Bujurg, Rajapakar, and Bhagwanpurs, Goraul, Patepur and Chehrakalan need three new colleges. High schools are sufficient in number in Raghopur anchal only. Other anchals need 5 to 11 additional schools. There should be a high schools on every 3 km. radius. Vaishali and Jandaha have sufficient primary schools. Other anchals need 10 to 30 more primary schools. The primary schools should be located at place where tiny tots do not have to cover more than 1 km.

Transportation and Communication :

Developed communication and Mass Media are essential for the development of human resource. The existing postal and communication services in the area is not satisfactory. Only about 14% villages are served by post and telegraph offices. There are 174 post offices and 19 telegraph offices in the area. The number of post offices required more in the Hajipur anchal is (4), Lalganj (5), Mahua (1), and Raghopur (1). Two additional telegraph offices should be established in Hajipur, Mahua and Raghopur each and one in Goraul, Patepur and Jandaha respectively. Besides these, all the Central villages should be provided with the facility of branch post offices.

Transportation facility is very important for the development of a region as the blood circulation for human body. In the areas only 26% of the villages are served by pucca road. All important places and anchals headquarters are connected through a network of all weather roads. But the interior villages are devoids of this facility. There is 1762 kms length of unmetalled roads, which became inoperatives during rainy season. These roads should be mettaled to make operative all around the year. Hajipur is the zone of East Central railway but 90% of the railway line in the area is single track which takes much time for covering small distances. These lines must be converted into double line tracks. River transport is negligible in the area. Some parts of Raghopur, Mahnar and Hajipur are connected thorugh river transportation with the capital Patna. If it is developed this could be cheapest tranportation facility for the farmers of Raghopur and Hajipur.

Madical facilties and Sanitation :

The indicators of good health are also the indicators of balanced development. In Vaishali health services are provided through government hospitals. Primary heatlh centres (PHC), Maternity and child welfare centre (MCWC) and family panning centres (FPC). But the number and functioning of these medical institutions are not satisfactory.

There is 23 more hospitals keep in the view growing population of the district. Goraul, Sahdai bujurg, Rabhopur, Chehra kalan, Desri, Bhagwanpur do not have big hospitals. One big hospital with all latest medical facilities should be established at these anchals. Hajipur and Mahua and 10 additional health centres each, Jandaha Mahnar, Patepur 4 each, Chehrakalan, Desri, Bhagwanpur need 2 each. These health centres should be establised at a place where it its easily accessible throughout the year.

(iii)Projection of human resource development : Birth, death and migration cause the change in the population structure of a region. The population growth of the area under study in alarmingly high. According to the census of 2001 Vaishali has a population of 27,12,389 which has 29.08% annual growth rate. Thus strong measures should be applied to control the population growth. It can be achieved to some extent, with the help of family planning. But due emphasiss will have given on the issue of raising the socio-ecónomic condition. Such as high marriage age, consciousness for small family (Hum Do Hamare do), nutrition level educational level, living standard etc. In our study region most people live in villages they believe childrens are Gods gift. They should not interfere in this. The avoid condom, oral, pills, sterilization, vasectomy, tubectomy, copper-T etc. because they feel it would make them weak and important. There is need for educating rural people by the NGO's and governmental agencies about Family planning. Small families should be given weightage in government services Bank loans and various government schemes such as Indira Awas Yojna, Jawahar Rojgar Yojna, IRDP, PMRY, KVC etc.

(iv) **Projection of Industrial development :** Projection related to the industrial development of the study region includes both invigoration of the sick and old industries and opening of the new one. This district is poor is industries due to lack of basic raw materials. But it is rich in agricultural resources. On the basis of these resources Infrastructure and the increasing demand, many industrial units may be established in different parts of the regions. Hajipur Industrial estate may be developed and units related to juice making, banana chips making, agricultural equipments making and other keep in view the local demands may be established. In other parts of the district also, agro based industries may be set up .This will ensure balanced regional development and increase employment opportunities in rural areas. The following steps should be taken in the form of industrial development project of the district :

(a) Small scale and cottage industries such as Iron grills, Steel furniture, rolling mills etc. be encouraged and set up at least at every block headquarters.

(b) Agro-based industries such as Iron, flour oil milling, gur making be promoted in every village having a populations of 1000 persons.

(c) One big centre each of dairy and poultry be set up at every subdivisional headquarters with its sub units at every block headquarters to meet the requirements of milk and egg of the growing population.

(d) Financial assistance be provided to the young and needy enterpreneurs for the construction of granary and cold storages wheres farmers can store their grains for selling them at proper time.

Thus on the basis of the above discussion it is clear that the agrobased industries at each and every block headquarters would go a long way to diversify the agriculture in its wake and prosperity of the inhabitants.

References :

1. Mishra, R.P. Sundaram, K.V. and Rao, V.L.S.P. (1974) : Regional development planning in India : A new strategy Vikas Publishing house Pvt. Ltd., p. 1.
2. Stamp, L.D. : Applied Geography, Penguin books.
3. Bennet, H.H. (1943) : Adjustment of agriculture in its environments, A.A.A. Geography, vol. 33-1, No.4, pp. 168-178.
4. Bihar government planning standards and building–by laws 1976.
5. Ibid.
6. Statistical data of Vaishali year 2001, Statistics Department of Vaishali, Hajipur.
7. Singh, L. (1982) : Rural Settlement Geography. A case study of Patna district U.B.B.P., Gorakhpur, p. 88.
8. Nath, V. (1961) : The growth of Indian agriculture : A regional analysis, the geographical review, vol. IX, No. 3.
9. Pandey, J.N. (1969) : Crop combination regions of U.P., Uttar Bharat Bhugol Patrika, vol. V, No. 1.
10. Prasad, M. (1974) : Agricultural Land Utilizations and nutrition : A case study of Bodh Gaya block (Gaya), Indian Geographical studies, Research bulletin, No. 3, September.

8

Planning The Countryside

Planning aspiring to raise the standards of living of its members. Every developed nation have resorted to systematic plan for better utilization of their resources and sustained economic growth. Planning is a cohesive exercise based on a broad vision. One must equally recognize that national priorities need not be the priorties at the micro level. District level planning assumes that planning has to incorporate the felt needs of the local people and the region covered. These needs differ from region to region. In other words each region should develop a blue print of its development taking into account the prevalent local conditions. Vaishali district with its 16 anchals and 93.33% rural inhabitants countryside planning poses a challenging task for the planners. They need an appropriate plan to meet the test of functionality, variability and administrative feasibility of the area.

Source: www.giz.de/static/en/images_content_460x160/815x459-Indien-Eng_rdax_460x259_80.jpg

Basic Principles of Planning :

A plan be formulated in way that it seem realistic and achievable in order to be successful. Simplification of procedures in necessary. A comprehensive compendium of rules and regulation be issued to be followed by the district administrative and N.G.O's as well.

There should be legislation relating to the redressal of public grievances which requires attention of the administration. The plan for the development of the countryside should tool after socio-economic development of the local people as well as local resources mobilization. The local people must effectively participate in planning, decision making, target fixing and implementation. On such mobilization hinges the success of planning which in turn demands a certain level of education in the society. This also necessitates. On such mobilization hinges the success of planning which in turn demands a certain level of education in the society. This also necessitates, among others, that the plan should be flexible and broadly framed to make it understandable to the common man. The area under study Vaishali district has mutipronged problems in countryside. It ranges from problems of wasteland, follows lands, irrigation, floods droughts, cropping pattern population pressure on land, unemployment, illiteracy problems of transport and communication, electricity, medical aid etc.

After viewing problems of Vaishali the plan for the countryside should address the areas of economic development as well as social and cultural development. Hence, the planning for this purpose must be grouped under the following heads. :

1. Planning for the agricultural development
2. Planning for development for socio-economic-Infrastructure.
3. Planning related to population pressure
4. Planning for industrial development.

Possible changes in General Landuse :

Land planning is in essence, the detemination of the optimums use of every hectare of land which must be elastic and change from time to time to adopt the changing condition. The present area under study Vaishali is a part of the middle Ganga plain. The land is almost flat and levelled with thick alluvium. There are about 62.30% area of the district is under Net sown Area. If follow lands are added to it, this comes to about 70% of the total area of the district. Rest of the land of the district is Non-arable accounting for about 30%. Out of which 12.62% of the land is barren and uncultivated wasteland, 16.21% of land is under the settlement and communication, cultivable waste land 0.18% permanent pastures 0.20% land under miscellaneous tree crops, grooves and orchards is 4.90%. There is no land under natural forest in the district.

The changes in recent landuse is a natural phenomena. According to heartshorne significant changes in landuse have been brought about by several imperceptible factors, as he observed "Non measurable but geographically significant phenomena must be studied indirectly by whatever measurable effects they have produced. However in Vaishali district the most important factor for bringing about landuse changes is the population which is growing at an alarming rate. Theory of study of landuse will not be complete if the changes which are taking place are not analysed. Thus, for the purpose of a comprehensive study of landuse, the changes must be studied and analysed carefully so that a purposeful planning with perfect decision may be drawn.

The spatial pattern of change in the Net sown area during 1991-2001 shows that a greater part of the district except the southern diara tract of Rahopur and Jandaha anchal of east central part has suffered loss in the Net sown area. This is an account of the very high rise in population pressure on agriculture land. Contrary to it, the Net sown area has registered an overall increase because other categories of land have also been put into use for agricultural purpose. Land put to non-agricultural uses is undergoing increase every day and every year because of rapidly rising population. The whole area except. North-Eastern section & southern section has recorded a positive change upto 20% of the land. The maximum change has been recorded in the diara tract of Raghopur and Patepur in both of these anchals the change has been upto 75%. Fallow lands are also increasing in all the parts of the district except central northern part north eastern part and east central part of the district following is a general practise among farmers for maintaining the fertility of the soil. Thus, Increase in follow land results into decrease of Net sown area. But there is an exception to this rule in the region.

In the southern part which is composed chiefly by the large tract of diara land of Raghopurs both Net sown area and follow lands have increased. This is because some parts of this diara land which were in the grip of meandring course of the river Ganga have also been reclaimed for cultivation of crops. Barren and uncultivable wastelands are being decreased year by year. These waste lands are being used for economical purposes. The Nothern part with an exception of the North-western sector has not witnessed any change. The central part has suffered a loss in this category of land. The Southern part except Bidupur anchal has gone under negative change. Thus, from above discussion on possible changes to take place in the future landuse pattern of the district can be calculated. It is apparent that on the one hand the Non-agricultural use of lands are on the rise on the other hand Net sown area is undergoing a decline. This is definitely on account of the increasing population pressure. The areas under current follow and cultivable waste land are increasing. It can be attributed to the increasing complexities brought about by the local problems including land disputes which are characteristics of an area having intense population pressure.

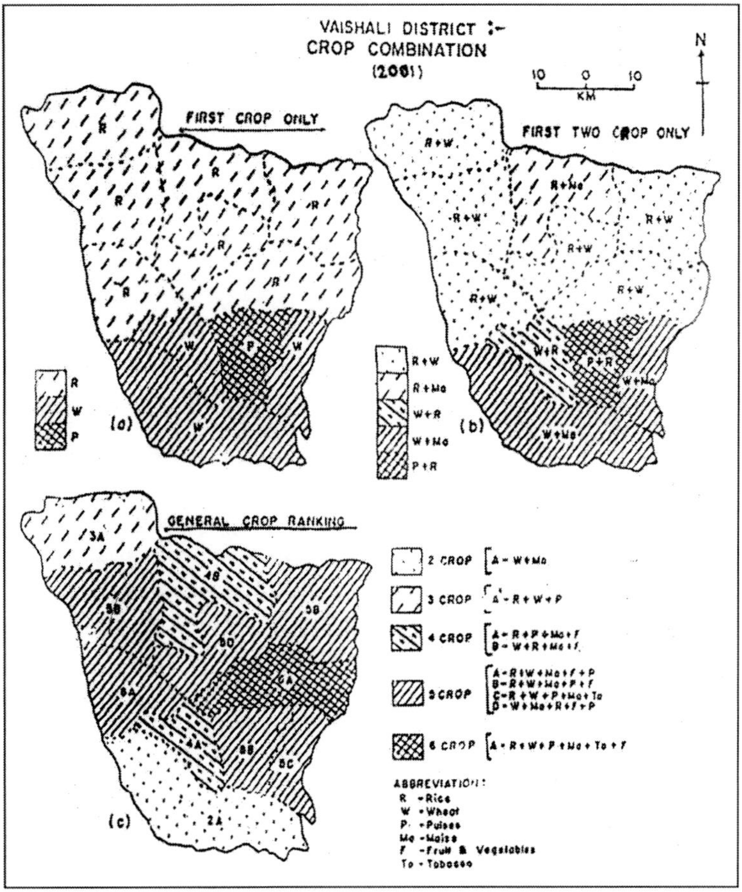
VAISHALI DISTRICT :-
CROP COMBINATION
N
KM
FIRST CROP ONLY
FIRST TWO CROP ONLY
GENERAL CROP RANKING
(a)
(b)
(c)
R
W
P
R+W
R+Ma
W+R
W+Ma
P+R
2 CROP A - W+Ma
3 CROP A - R+W+P
4 CROP A - R+P+Ma+F B - W+R+Ma+F
5 CROP A - R+W+Ma+F+P B - R+W+Ma+P+F C - R+W+P+Ma+To D - W+Ma+R+F+P
6 CROP A - R+W+P+Ma+To+F
ABBREVIATION:
R - Rice
W - Wheat
P - Pulses
Ma - Maize
F - Fruit & Vegetables
To - Tobacco

Fig. 8.1

Changes in Crop distribution :

The region where the main occupation of the people is farming and where a variety of crop are grown owing to favourable geographical factors. The most suitable method to divide the whole region in to smaller regions is to delineate the crop distribution regions. It is one of the techniques of agricultural regionalization and forms a fundamental part in the study of geography which is mainly related to spatio-temporal analysis of phenomena. Agricultural regionalization is essential because of it is intemetely connected with the eradication of agricultural backwardness by rational allocation of new enterprises. A region is always transitional in character since it can not be demarcated by boundaries which may serve also as the administrative boundaries. An agricultural region changes gradually into another region. Thus it becomes very difficult task for a geographer to delimit the boundaries of an agricultural region.

In Vaishali district the physical as well as climatic factors are most suitable for the cultivation of a varieties of crop. The land has been used extensively and intensively for the cultivation of various crops. During a span of ten years 1991-2001 some variations in the distribution of crops in different anchals have been observed. So far as only the first crop is concerned there is little variation. Changes have occureed in the anchals of Sahdai Bujurg and Desri where the ratio of pulses which was highest has been shifted to Vaishali anchal. In Sahdai Bujurg paddy has taken place of pulses. In the two crop combination regions it is again observed that there has been little variation during the period of 1991-2001. The combination of paddy+wheat which is found in eight anchals has increased to ten anchals in 1991-2001. It points towards a greater stress on the cultivation of basic foodcrops. In the remaining six anchals minor changes being observed. The change noticeable has been found in the cultivation of pulses which has been replaced by paddy as the number one crop in Vaishali and has been shifted to second crop with wheat in Mahnar.

Table 8.1
Vaishali District
Crop distribution regions

No. of Crops	Crop combination	No. of Anchal's	Anchal's name
Two crop	Wheat+maize	1	Raghopur
Three crop	Paddy+wheat+pulses	2	Desri, Jandaha
Four crops	Paddy+wheat+ maize +fruits and vegetables	4	Mahua, Raja Pakar, Patheri Belsar, Sahdai Bujurg
Five crops	Wheat+paddy+maize & vegetables+pulses	5	Lalganj, Bidupur, Vaishali, Mahnar, Hajipur
Six crops	Paddy+wheat+pulses +maize+Tobacco+	4	Goraul , Bhagwanpur, Chehra kalan, Patepur.

Source : Based on figures available from the directorate of statistics and evalution. Govt. of Bihar, Patna.

The changes in general crop ranking during period 1981-1991 reflect a greater degree of diversification of agricultural crops. In 1991-2001 the combination of two crops and four crops which were in existence in 1981-1991 have lost their place in 1991-2001. The combination of five crops has witnessed the maximum increase since it has extended its area from six anchals to eight anchals in 1991-2001.

The above discussion on changes in crop distribution suggest that even thought the food like paddy and wheat have sustained greater attention due to fast growing population, the farmers at the sametime are also paying their greater attention towards the cultivation of other crops like pulses, tobaccco, fruits and vegetables in order to balance their economy. This is a good sign indicating improvement in agriculture. The change also suggest towards some degree of commercialization and specialization may take place which will brighten the agricultural prospects and will also open new avenues for agricultural development in the Vaishali district.

Problems of Wasteland and potential use of land :

Today about 175 million hectares of about 329 million hectares of the country's land is threatened by various types of land degradation and leading to ever increasing depletion of productivity.

Wonton misuse has led to the poor healths of soil and land resources and an impoverished environment. Many areas fit to be cultivations have been lost annually throught mining and encroachment of ravines. There has been also significant increase of wastelands due to water logging, salinity and desertification because of the retrogression of vegetation.

The region under study Vaishali has a vast area under wastelands. It covers an area of about 60,722 hectares accounting for 12.80% of the total area of the district. It is higher than the average ratio for Bihar (6.93%). These lands are mostly found in the vast sandy diara tracts. The spatial pattern of this category of land in 2001 shows that the southern part of the district has maximum wastelands. Some of the anchals which has wasteland areas are Hajipur, Lalganj, Patepur, Mahua, Desri, Mahnar and Goraul. These anchals have wastelands mainly because of its low lying area, which are flooded every year by the river Gandak and river Ganga. There are westlands. Due to water logging, crops are not produced in water prone areas of Vaishali district.

Potential use of Wasteland :

Wastelands of Vaishali District could be used in following ways. These lands should be used for vegetable cultivation because it requires less time for ripening and it has ready market demand in the state capital Patna. Other crops which may be cultivated in these lands are Maize, sugarcane, Jowar, Bajra and broadcast paddy. There is a department of wastelands developments under the Ministry of Rural Developments which started many schemes for the reclamation and development of these lands. They aim towards upliftment of living standards of people through employment generation. They provide some variety of trees to be cultivated in these areas. These tree give fodder for animals, wood for house, furniture etc. Some NGO's are also active in these areas. They are involveds in sand extraction, fish catching and river transportation. But these are not enough Government must give extra attention to these areas and provide aid for the development of socio-economic condition of the inhabitatants. The rivers of these areas are full of debris. Their depth has become almost equal to the ground level. It these rivers are dug out and its banks made higher the scare of flood would be minimized. Their should also made canals system which may be used for irrigation and water management of the area, Government should ensure people's participation and involvement of Panchayat's and voluntary agencies for the farming of 'Jatropha' a bio-diesel tree. The Indian farmers, Fertilizer cooperative, the largest fertilizer manufacturing group, promoted a new cooperative society to implement the concept of farm forestry for wasteland development. IFFCO itself is a cooperative promoted by various district and state-level farmers cooperatives and it provides an array of farming related services, including seeds production and wasteland development. It has successfully demonstrated a cooperative approach to wasteland developments by organizing marginal farmerss into primary societies to take up farm forestry on their unproductives land. Other government agencies such as CAPART and NABARD could emulate IFFCO's efforts in the wasteland development through a comprehensive programme for the development of socio-economic status of the people living in these areas. More and more initiatives need to be taken by the state govt. on many fronts so that the land mass of the distirct becomes more productive and is put to its optional use. Only then the rural people of the area would be able to benefit from land reform measures and activities pertaining to rural development.

References :

1. Mishra, R.P. Sundaram, K.V. and Rao, V.L.S.P. (1974) : Regional development planning in India : A new strategy Vikas Publishing house Pvt. Ltd. p. 5.
2. Bennet, H.H. (1943) : Adjustment of agriculture in its environments, A.A.A. Geography, vol. 33-1, No. 4, pp. 169-180.
3. Ibid.
4. Stamp, L.D. (1960) : In the forward of "The changing use of land in Britain."
5. Singh Jasbir and Dhillon, S.S. : Agricultural Geography, Tata Mcgraw Hill Ltd. New Delhi, 1982.
6. Navin Chandra Joshi : Wastelands Development; Land reform as a tool, Civil services chronicle magazine, December 1999 issue.
7. Athavale, A.G. (1966) : "Some new methods of crop combination" Geographical review in India, vol. XXVII, No. 3.
8. Chatterjee, S.P. (1941) : "The place of Geography in national planning", Calcutta geographical review, vol.3.
9. Jha, B.N. (1965) : "Land capability classification of the Kosi region, geographical outlook, vol. XX.
10. Hussain, M. (1994) : Human Geography, Rawat Publication, New Delhi.
11. Singh, R.P. (2007) : Rural Development and Panchayati Raj in India; Janaki Prakashan, Patna.

9

Summary and Conclusion

The purpose of the present study is to analyse the level of natural, economic and human resources and its role in the rural area development. After finding out the association between natural, economic and human resources and rural development, the measuress for the rural area development have been suggested. For the study Vaishali district has been selected as a case study. This district is very rich in natural and economic resources but low level of rural development has been caused by improper utilization of natural as well as human resources.

A humble attempt has been made in present study to interperete the patten and level of rurals development in the Vaishali district of Bihar. Rural development in influenced by several factors such as physical, techological and institutional factors. Some prominent phenomena of the district rural areas are decreasing per capita land, increasing population pressure on land, increasing irrigation facilities and modern implement's use, use of fertilizers and hybrid seeds. Agrobased industries growth, development of growth centres, changes in cropping pattern and lands utilizations etc.

The study is based on collection of data and maps supplemented by feild work and analysis of data and maps. Sample survey has also been undertaken to have first hand information regarding the present status of rural development in the study area.

Most of the data have been collected from the districts statistics office, Vaishali Hajipur which have been supplemented by census report and annuals action plan prepared by the lead bank. Maps have been procured from the government press, Gulzarbagh feild surveys were conducted for investigating the various aspects of rural development. Data and map analysis are based on modern techinques. The present study consists of Nine chapters including summary.

Vaishali district is located between 25°29'N and 26°1'N latitudes, and 85°4'E and 85°36'E longitudes in the southern part of North Bihar plain at the confluence of the rivers Ganga and Gandak. It is joined with Patna and Chhapra through bridges. All vehicles coming from south Bihar to north Bihar pass through the Mahatma Gandhi setu over the Ganga located on the Barauni–Hajipur chord line and Muzaffapur–Hajipur Trunk lines the district headquarter Hajipur has been made the zonal headquarter of the East Central Railway.

Physiographically the district is formed of the alluviums brought by the rivers draining it. It is a dead level plain having an average elevation of 50 meters above the sea level and a general slope from north-west to south-east. It is characterized by many ox-bow lakes, locally called "Chaurs" eg. Tal baraila and diara tract. Main rivers of the area under study are the Ganga, the Gandak, the baya, and the Nun. These rivers are useful for irrigation and transport.

By the sight of climate this region lies in the transitional zone between the moist West Bengal and dry western U.P. as it is open to free flow of easterly and westerly winds. The summers season in marked by high temperature and dust winds having occasional thunder showers. Rainfall is maximum in the north-east from where it decreases towards the west, average annual rainfalll being 180 cm in the former and 100 cm in the latter. July and August recieve maximum rainfall. January is the coldest month having a minimum of 10°c temperature. Winter is characterized by one or two spells of rainfall caused by temperate cyclonic winds. These climatic characteristics have a great bearing on the pattern of agriculture.

The region is covered by Gangetic alluvium divisible into new alluvium or 'khadar' and old alluvium or 'bhangar'. Bhangar is an upland soil and it is mostly loamy, but it grades from sandy to clayey loam. Khadar is limited to the low lands; it is rich in plantfood particularly Nitrogen and is less calcarious and carbonic than bhangar. It is suitable for rice cultivation. The eastern Saryupur and Central western North Bihar plains have calcarious soil rich in lime and the best suited to the cultivation of sugarcane. The Tarai area has heavy clayey soil suitable for rice cultivation.

The land being fertile, no area is left for wild growth of vegeation. However, moist deciduous group of trees such as Mango, Litchi, Jackfruit, Mahua, Banyan and Pipal trees are found here. It has young alluvial calcarious soil having regional variation. Sandy soil is found in Raghopur diara, Loamy soil in upland area and clayey soil in low lying area.

Vaishali is spread over an area of 2036 sq.kms and has 27,12,389 persons according to 2001 census. Since 1881 it has experienced variation in growth of population, a very slow increase during 1881-1911, a decline during 1911-1921, a slow growth during 1921-1951 and a rapid growth during 1951-2001. The previous decade 1991-2001 has experienced the highest increase of 26.38% in its population. The district has a very high density of 1332 persons per sq.kms. But the distribution of population is very uneven. Hajipur, Lalganj, and Bidupur has high concentration of population where as Raghopur, Patepur and Vaishali have comparatively sparse population.

The level of literacy in the district is very low at only 40.82% Raghopur anchal has even 26.02% literates. Hajipur, Bidupur, Lalganj, Mahnar and Sahdai Bujurg have comparatively high literacy 45%-50%. The averages sex ratio is also very low 958, while it is 921 for Bihar. 20% of the people belong to schedule castes, while schedule tribes are negligible in number.

As regards occupational structure of population, 86% of

the mains workers belong to primary group having cultivators 49% agricultural labourers 38%, Raghopur anchal has the highest percentage of cultivators and Goraul has the lowest.

Landuse is the most dominant form of resource utilization. Vaishali district presents a diverse type of landuse because some parts have higher ground, some contain lower ground while some are fertile and others are not. Mainly landuse categories of Vaishali could be Net sown area 62.30%, Land put to Non-agricultural use 16.21%, current fallow 3.31%, Barren and uncultivated land 12.62%, other fallow 0.28%, land under miscelleneous trees and grooves 4.90%. cultivable waste 0.18%, permanents pasture and other grazing land is 0.20%. Net sown areas are land under cropping. Land category put to non-agricultural use are inhabiteds areas and these lands are used for hospital, school, houses, Bus station, markets, water bodies etc. Current fallow lands are left for the region of soil nutreints and are used in the next crop season. All the above categories of land uses can be brought into two major classes, viz. arable and Non-arable. Arable group includes the Net sown area, current fallow and other fallow lands. Non arable group includes the rest categories of uses.

The type and quality of the soil of an area is major factor in land Utilization. In Vaishali district three broads land types can be recognized. These are class I lands, Class II lands and Class III lands. Class I land are close to settlements sites and high costly. These lands are fit for settlements while class II and III lands are fit only for agricultural purpose.

There are four agricultural harvests in the district. These are Bhadai, Aghani, Rabi and Garma corresponding to early monsoon, Late monsoon, spring and summer seasons. In each harvest a number of crops are grown so that the agricultural scenery changes from season to season. Two or, more succesive crops are obtained from the same filed. Farmers usually practice a sorts of crop rotation to get the maximum return from the fields. Rabi crops are the most significant accounting for 38% of the total cropped area. Aghani crops are grown over 28%, Garma over 20% and Bhadai over 13% of the cropped land. Rabi crops are more significant in Raghopur, Sahdai Bujurg and Hajipur aghani crops in Sahdai Bujurg, Vaishali and Patepur Garma crops in Bidupur. Mahnar and Hajipur and Bhadai crops is high in Sahdai Bujurg, Mahua, Lalganj and Mahnar and low in Vaishali and Hajipur. The diversity of cropping is more pronounced in Sahdai Bujurg, Bidupur and Mahnar.

Paddy, wheat, maize, mung, vegetables, banana and oilseeds are the principle crops of Vaishali district. These crops are grown in different seasons of agricultural years. There are some crops which are grown in more than one harvest. Yet, different seasons have their own significant crop. Among Rabi crops, wheat is the single most significant crop. Other Rabi crops are maize, vegetables, pulses and oilseeds. Among Garma crops mung is the most significant followed by Maize, banana, vegetables and paddy. Paddy is the most important among aghani crops, vegetables are also grown druing aghani season. Maize is the most important Bhadai crop followed by paddy, vegetables, marua, Jute and urad.

There is regional variation in the area under different crops. In Aghani paddy mahua, Patepur and Lalganj are significant while in Bhadai paddy Goraul Patepur and Mahua hold the same place. These for anchals are also significant in the area under wheat. Bhadai Maize is significant in Mahua, Jandaha and Vaishali Rabi Maize in Patepur, Raghopur and Goraul and Garma maize in Goraul, Patepur and Jadaha. In the production the production of Mung Goraul, Patepur and Jandaha. In the production the production of Mung Goraul, Mahua, Patepur and Jandaha are important. In Rabi potato also these anchals are significant. In the pulse production Mahua, Lalganj and Jandaha are important, while in Banana Bidupur and Hajipur are by far the most significant. In Rabi oilseeds Mahua, Lalganj and Hajipur are important. In this way there is a spatial variation in the production of different crops. In respect of area covered by different crops paddy is the most important followed by wheat, maize, potato, mung, pulse, banana, oilseeds, marua and Barley in that order. But in production wheat is most important followed by Rice, potato, maize, banana, mung in that order. Growth centres of the district Vaishali are its sixteen anchals which are centre of political and administrative activities, Agrobased industries, local market place for agricultural products, education facilities, Health and hospitals facilities and cultural activities etc. Among anchals Vaishali is the most ancient Growth centre from which the district derives its name. It is the birth place of democratic form of government 'the Lichhavi' state was the first of its king Vaishali is the holy place for Hindus, Jainies and Buddhist and hence it is a very significant place. It is connected to the state capital Patna by Mahatma Gandhi Setu. It is the administrative headquarter of the district. The east railway has established its zonals headquarter here.

Bases of rural development could be categorized into two broad groups :

(a) Economic development and

(b) Socio-cultural development

Economic development comprises Industrial development as well as Agricultural efficiency. While socio-cultural development includes literacy, health facilties, social and caste stigmas etc. Analysis of Vaishali district on these to parameters suggests that it is a backward district and there is potentiality for rural development. Effort are needed by the state government of promote educational facilities, health facilities, scientific method of agriculture and means of transport and communications in a proper planned way. Any region should develop a blue print of its developments taking into account the local needs and its resources.

After viewing the problems of Vaishali district the plan for the countryside must address the areas of economic as well as, social and cultural development. Hence, the planning for this purpose be grouped under the following heads :

(1) Planning for the agricultural development.

(2) Planning for development of socio-economic infrastucture.

(3) Planning related to population pressure.

(4) Planning for Industrial development.

The recent changes in crop distribution suggests that even though foodcrops like paddy and wheat have sustained greater attention, due to fast growing population's feeding needs farmers at the sametime are also paying attention towards the cultivation of other cash crops like pulses, tobacco, fruits and vegetables in order to balance their economy. This is a good sign indicating improvement in agriculture.

The are under study Vaishali has a vast area under wasteland. It covers an area of about 60,722 hectares accounting for 12.80% of the total area of the district. Most of the wastelands are situated in the low lying areas of Mahnar, Patepur, Mahua, Desri, Goraul and Raghopur anchals. For the reclamations and development of these lands social forestry could be an easy solution. NGO's Gram panchayats and co-operatives could cultivate Jatrapha (Biodiesel plant), Bamboo, Bent and other wood producing plants which are useful for making furniture and houses. Pisciculture could also flourish in these lands. Government Agencies such as NABARD and CAPART also provide financial support to various projects in these areas.